WINGS OF FREEDOM

Peter Walley

Nigel Weir

Sandy Lane

David Crook

Victor Beamish

Cowboy Blatchford

Richard Hillary

Michael Robinson

Eric Marrs

Paterson Hughes

Willie Rhodes-Moorhouse

John Dundas

By the same author:
DOUBLE MISSION:
RAF Fighter Ace and SOE Agent Manfred Czernin, DSO, MC, DFC
FIGHTER LEADER:
The Story of Wing Commander Ian Gleed, DSO, DFC, CdeG
THE GREATEST AIR BATTLE:
Dieppe, 19th August 1942

WINGS
OF FREEDOM

Twelve Battle of Britain Pilots

Norman L. R. Franks

WILLIAM KIMBER · LONDON

First published in 1980 by
WILLIAM KIMBER & CO. LIMITED
Godolphin House, 22a Queen Anne's Gate,
London, SW1H 9AE

Photoset by
Specialised Offset Services, Liverpool
and printed in Great Britain by
Redwood Burn, Limited, Trowbridge and Esher

Contents

List of Illustrations

Acknowledgements

I wish to thank Mrs Diana Fawkes for permission to use the letters of her brother Nigel Weir, and to C.P.O. Bartlett DSC for his recollections of Nigel. I am also most grateful to Wing Commander T.F. Neil DFC AFC for his recollections of Victor Beamish.

I am grateful to *Aeroplane Monthly* for permission to quote from issues of the *Aeroplane*, 1945, for the story of Eric Marrs. I would also like to thank Messrs Faber & Faber for permission to quote from *Verses of a Fighter Pilot* by Nigel Weir; to Souvenir Press for *Lonely Warrior* edited by Victor Houart, and to MacMillan & Co. Ltd., for *The Last Enemy* by Richard Hillary. Thanks are also due to my friend Chaz Bowyer, the Imperial War Museum, Public Records Office, and to the staff at William Kimber & Co. Also to Bill Miles who helped with the research into Peter Walley's life. Finally, as always to my family: my wife Kate and sons Rob and Mike.

Introduction

Following the fall of France in 1940 and the withdrawal of the British Expeditionary Force from Dunkirk, Britain stood alone against the might of Germany. Just a tiny strip of water, the English Channel, sat like a barrier against Hitler's armies. All that was needed was for the German Air Force, a victorious Luftwaffe which had paved the way for victories in Spain, then Poland, Norway and now France and the Low Countries, to gain air superiority above the Channel and southern England. If he could win that superiority, Hitler believed that Britain would either surrender, or he could invade and truly dominate the whole of Europe.

His only real problem was the Royal Air Force. In comparison to his Luftwaffe, the RAF, or specifically Fighter Command, numbered very few. At the time when what has become known as the Battle of Britain, was about to begin, Fighter Command only had between 600 to 700 single-seater fighter aircraft – less than 50 squadrons. The Luftwaffe had over 2,200 aircraft. Royal Air Force fighter pilots totalled 1,253, 197 short of establishment. With these, Fighter Command's AOC, Air Chief Marshal Hugh Dowding, had to defend the whole of the British Isles. It was these men, Churchill's famous 'Few' that would stop Hitler's dream of conquest and total victory.

*

Forty years after the momentous battle, fought in a hot summer sky over southern England from July to October 1940, people's imagination is still fired by the exploits of those involved. In this book we look at just twelve of the men who helped to make, were part of, history. Fighting daily against great odds with the tenacious ferocity that epitomizes the British when their backs are against the wall, these twelve are merely a representative handful of the 'Few'.

So, why did I choose these twelve? Two themes I have pursued.

Firstly I wanted to record the writings that some of them left for us, whether in book form, letters or notations in flying log-books. Secondly, and this also embraces the first, I was interested in recording in some detail the lives of some of the lesser known pilots, or to be more correct, to expand on a name which often rang a bell in the memory but left questions about what else that man achieved or what happened to him.

I was often intrigued about what happened to Brian Lane, who wrote the book *Spitfire*, and to David Crook who wrote *Spitfire Pilot*. In researching them I also discovered that their log-books survive. I was equally sure that Richard Hillary's story was worth looking at clinically to see exactly what he achieved during the battle before he wrote his famous book *The Last Enemy*. Eric Marrs' published letters and Nigel Weir's unpublished letters are worth writing about for they contain the very essence of what Battle of Britain pilots were all about. I also wanted to know more about others. What exactly did the great Victor Beamish do in 1940? What else did John Dundas do before meeting and shooting down Helmut Wick, then dying with the yell of victory on his lips? What did Cowboy Blatchford achieve in addition to helping to rout the Italians? And what about Peter Walley, who crashed and died just a quarter of a mile from where I now live?

In answering these questions it was necessary to read the squadrons' diaries, read the flyers' log-books where they survive, and read their actual combat reports. The result, I hope, is a record of bravery showed by each of the twelve in various ways.

Forgetting for a moment the buzz and drone of aircraft, the white condensation trails against the backdrop of summer blue, the high, distant rattle of machine-guns, let us look at the daily actions of these men. We can read of the tactics used, be a part of the twisting, turning dog-fights and the lone chases against the single raiders; the awe-inspiring sight of vast air armadas and the fights against tremendous odds, and the loss of dear friends. All of this is part of their story – the Few's story.

This is not just another book about the Battle of Britain, it is a book about twelve men who fought in it and who either failed to survive that great conflict or the total catastrophe that was the Second World War.

NORMAN FRANKS Morden, Surrey.

1

Peter

Courage and personal heroism show themselves in many ways during war. The vast majority of Britain's pilots who fought in the summer sky of 1940 displayed these qualities almost daily. The mere act of scrambling into the air to fight an enemy of superior numbers was an act of courage in itself. On occasions, however, a single moment of decision, a lone moment in time, had to be faced. The decision often meant the difference between life and death, sometimes for the man himself, sometimes for others. Peter's story embraced both. The decision for him, his moment in time, his personal act of courage meant either life or death for him so that others would not be endangered. For this young man, still three months away from his twenty-first birthday, the decision, the act, had to be faced, an act very very few young men today have to face and decide upon.

Peter Kenneth Walley was born on 20 November 1919 in Barnes, south-west London. His father had served in the Great War, firstly with the Machine Gun Corps and later as a lieutenant in the Tank Corps. The family moved to Sutherland Grove, Southfields (near Wimbledon), Peter attending school in Sutherland Grove. He was keen on sport, an able swimmer and captain of the rugger team.

His father died when Peter was thirteen years old and he and his mother moved to a flat in Croydon. Even as a small boy he was interested in flight and flying, making model aeroplanes in his spare time. When he left school, his mother had him apprenticed to a tool-makers firm in Croydon (his father had been a London rep for Spear & Jackson). Yet his main interest centred on the air and progressed beyond the building of model aeroplanes, so much so, that in March 1938 he enlisted as an aircrafthand/air gunner in the Royal Auxiliary Air Force, spending his weekends in this capacity. In August 1938 he became part of No 615 Squadron RAuxAF. When war came, he left his apprenticeship and at the end of the year his wish to become a pilot was realised. He already had considerable experience in the air when selected for pilot training which enabled him to quickly complete training courses at No's 3 and 5 Flying Training Schools; he finally received his coveted RAF 'wings' on 11 July 1940, just as the Battle of Britain was beginning.

Two days later he was posted back to 615 Squadron but this time as a fully-fledged pilot. He arrived, following a short leave, on 6 August. The squadron was commanded by Squadron Leader J.R. Kayll, flew Hawker Hurricane fighters and was stationed at RAF Kenley in Surrey.

Any pilot on the strength of a front line fighter squadron in 1940, however new and untried, had to be numbered among its ranks. In periods of calm the novice pilot might be able to take advantage of the time to increase his flying experience, add valuable flying hours to his log, listen and learn from his seniors. However, 615 Squadron, along with others in 11 Group Fighter Command, was about to enter what was in fact the Luftwaffe's main assault against England and her Royal Air Force.

The very next day following his arrival, Peter Walley took Hurricane P2963 on patrol immediately after lunch. Two days later a dawn patrol. On the 10th the squadron flew several patrols in the afternoon from Kenley and Hawkinge, the latter being 615's forward base. Peter flew a total of three hours on this Saturday afternoon – an afternoon of frustrations due mainly to bad weather.

A late afternoon patrol on the 11th (in P2966) proved fruitless, but 615 had been in action earlier that day, although Walley was not involved. In that earlier fight the squadron had lost two pilots killed in action with JG26 and had another Hurricane shot-up. In the late morning of the 15th, Walley flew N2328 on patrol. 615 was again in action with German fighters, losing another pilot killed with another wounded. The next afternoon Peter (in P2871) was in action against German bombers, Heinkel 111s of KG27 and KG55, escorted by Me110 fighters. 615, in company with Hurricanes from 1 Squadron and Spitfires of 64 Squadron engaged them.

Six-one-five took off from Kenley at eighteen minutes past four o'clock. In the air they were ordered to intercept and engage Raid No 15 which was at that moment approaching Brighton from the south. Over this famous seaside town, at four minutes to five, the enemy was seen, flying at 18,000 feet. They consisted of two large

Peter Walley

formations of Heinkels, forty to fifty in each formation flying in large vics in line astern. Up above, stepped up and to the rear flew several groups of twin-engined Messerschmitts.

The squadron attacked, Peter Walley flying as Number Two to Squadron Leader Kayll who was Red Leader. Kayll attacked the rear section of bombers picking out one aircraft and opened fire from the rear at 300 yards' range. Keeping his thumb down he let go a 15-second burst. Smoke and vapour poured from the German's port motor, and the propeller slowed up, but then Kayll's windscreen became covered in oil from the crippled bomber. Walley then closed in on the Heinkel, getting in several bursts at 300 and 250 yards. The Heinkel went into clouds below still smoking and in Walley's opinion, the German went into the sea just off Brighton.

Meanwhile the other pilots in the squadron were in amongst the bombers; Pilot Officer C.R. Young sent one into the sea ten miles south east of Bognor; Pilot Officer K.T. Lofts hit another which dived through the clouds. Keith Lofts followed to see the bomber glide down to a crash landing near Steyning. Other pilots claimed damaging hits on other Heinkels and some 110s were also hit when they came down and joined in. The squadron landed back at Kenley shortly after six pm.

The following day, the 17th, was comparatively quiet, both sides in the battle taking a breather following the previous few days' intense fighting. In the previous eight days, Fighter Command had suffered more than 100 pilot casualties, 78 of whom had been killed. Many had been experienced men, hard to replace. It was a tense period.

On Sunday, 18 August the battle was resumed. The German Luftwaffe was still desperately trying to knockout the RAF and its southern airfields. The morning was quiet, not until about mid-day did the radar screens begin to pick-up signs of approaching raiders. At Kenley, 615 were ordered up at 12.47 pm to intercept Raid No 45, the enemy being sighted in the Kenley area at about 1 o'clock. They consisted of Dornier 17s and Ju88s in large numbers, escorted by the everpresent fighters high above. The bombers were in large vic formations at 10-12,000 feet, and the fighters between 26-30,00 feet.

Mr Willis, an NCO at Kenley, remembered that day:

As I was coming from the stores there was a big flap on. Peter came dashing out of one of the huts with his his helmet and R/T lead in his hand yelling, 'Start me up somebody!' A few moments later, with a burst of throttle and a cloud of dust, he taxied out of the aircraft pen and across the field to catch up with the others. A few moments later with a shattering roar that made the windows rattle in the huts, 615's Hurricanes were racing across the airfield and up over the boundary. Peter had caught them up and was getting into the Number 3 position in Yellow Section, soon to be lost in the haze; 'Panter' Squadron was airborne.

RAF Biggin Hill, only a short distance from Kenley, was first to be attacked as nine Dorniers from KG76 bombed at low level. Then it was Kenley's turn. 615 Squadron overhead were, however, attacked by the German escort. Number 3 in Blue Section was Pilot Officer D.J. Looker, flying L1592 KW-Z:

We were ordered to patrol Hawkinge and while we were climbing, were re-ordered to turn north-east and keep a look out for fighters in the area. One section of Hurricanes had difficulty in keeping up with the formation and gradually fell behind, finally being lost in the haze. We were at 26,000 feet with the sun behind us when the 109s hit us. I suddenly saw Walley's Hurricane getting hit and start smoking. It turned right over and went down. I was being attacked myself [and] too busy to see exactly what happened to Walley. My own aircraft was badly damaged, taking several cannon shells in the wings, tail and fuselage. I managed to force-land on Croydon aerodrome, with the airfield defences firing at me in error as I came in.[1]

Pilot Officer P.H. 'Dutch' Hugo (later Group Captain DSO DFC and two bars) saw the attack, saw a Messerschmitt slide in behind Walley who was on the extreme starboard side of the formation. Hugo yelled a warning over the R/T but it was already too late.

[1] Looker's Hurricane can today be seen in the Science Museum in London.

The exact extent of the damage to Peter Walley's machine is not known. David Looker saw it smoking and another report states it going down in flames. However, any fire or heavy smoke had died away considerably when he was seen down at a lower altitude. This is confirmed by several eye witnesses from the ground. One of these was a ten year old boy, Bill Miles:

It was about mid-day when the distant rumble of aircraft grew nearer like a vast formation making a dull roar which seemed to surround one and beat on the eardrums. Neighbours working in their gardens, and passers-by, stopped and looked skywards shading their eyes with their hands as the noise grew louder. Then we saw them. They seemed to be in every bit of the sky to the east of us, several large formations of twin-engined aircraft in wide vic formations in line astern. Then we spotted the fighter escort – there seemed to be hundreds of them, leaving short vapour trails. About 3/10ths cloud prevented us from seeing all.

'Too many to be our boys,' one neighbour said. He was right too, for then the sirens went. [My friend] Raymond ran home and my mother called me inside.

Local AA guns started firing, making black and white puffs in the sky. We hadn't an air-raid shelter at the time, so were invited to share the Anderson shelter of the Lacy Family next door. Mr Bert Lacy and elder son Fred gave us a running commentary on what was happening outside and then Bert said,

'Our boy's up there; go on give it to them German B——!' I just had to see this. I pushed and squeezed my way to the shelter entrance nearly getting debagged by my mother in her efforts to stop me, but she too was held by the sight we saw. Vapour trails, British and German were everywhere. We could also hear the distant whine of diving aircraft and rattle of machine-gun fire, seeing untidy lines of twisting and turning aircraft looking like minute golden crosses as the sun caught them as they turned.

There was a big battle going on over the Wimbledon/Merton area, to the north east of us and we counted four parachutes suspended in the middle of it, also a black smoke trail from a burning aircraft disappearing behind a bank of cloud. There was another battle going on also to the south-east and there was also a white vapour trail turning gradually to a black trail but going too near to that hazy glare of the sun, that we couldn't really tell for sure what happened to it.

Suddenly a Hurricane hurtled from out of that glittering haze, cleared the high tension cables which ran almost parallel to the Sutton By-Pass, and then at roof-top height flew right across the St Helier Estate turning slightly to the left, disappearing behind the rooftops. He then came into view again climbing, and now turning steeply to the right as if to avoid a last minute crash into houses on the London Road. The nose of the aircraft went down and it disappeared from view, the sound of the crash that followed confirmed its fate. A short while later the 'All Clear' sounded and every one came out and looked at the pillar of black smoke as it rolled across the estate where, but for the bravery in riding it down, his wrecked plane could have been, with the loss of life which usually follows, but with him suspended safely in his parachute harness.

Mr Hall was walking along the London Road with his father at the same time:

As soon as I saw the aircraft I knew it was a Hurricane. It was coming from the direction of St Helier in a shallow dive with its engine just ticking over, and just cleared a row of houses on the London Road near Holne Chase. I remember it carried no nationality markings under the wings and the seemingly huge oil-spattered, soot-streaked undersides, as it swept over my head about forty feet up. It brushed the tall trees on the edge of Morden Park, on the other side of the road, and although dangerously low and almost certainly controls limp with lack of airspeed, went into a steep right bank. It seemed to miss a clump of trees in its path further in the park, then the fighter lost airspeed completely and went down, smashing into more trees, knocking one down which wrenched off the right wing as it hurtled on for 25 yards disintegrating and scattering lots of blazing petrol, setting a poultry farm and some dog kennels on fire. The pilot was killed instantly.

*

In the clash above, 615 Squadron had been hit savagely by Me109s from JG3. Apart from Walley and Looker being hit by 109s, Red Leader, Flight Lieutenant L.M. Gaunce's machine (P2966) was set on fire at 20,000 feet forcing him to bale out. Dutch Hugo too had to leave his shattered Hurricane (R4221), and was slightly wounded, ending up in Orpington Hospital. On the credit side the squadron claimed one Heinkel 111, two Dorniers and a Junkers 88 destroyed, an Me109 and a Dornier probably destroyed plus two fighters and two bombers damaged.

On the airfield at Kenley 615 Squadron had six of its Hawker Hurricanes destroyed in the bombing and one officer was killed when a bomb hit the slit-trench in which he was taking cover. Two LACs were hit, one being killed instantly, the other being so badly injured that he died two days later.

Meanwhile, local residents around Morden were starting to gather on Morden Park where Peter Walley's machine had crashed. Bill Miles was one of them:

Later I was allowed to go and see where it had crashed, so we just walked towards the smoke, joining the crowds going there most of them thinking it was a German plane. It was still burning when we got there and every so often a few rounds of ammunition would go off which kept people at a respectful distance. A tree was knocked over with its leaves and branches everywhere and a wing laying beside it, the burnt out fuselage was about 25 yards further on with the other wing nearby. The engine had made a small crater and it and the nose were smashed from the fuselage.

There is little doubt by all those who witnessed it that Peter Walley had stayed with his machine in order to avoid its crashing into the built-up area over which he was fighting. It would have been so easy for him to have baled out and saved himself, but obviously that was not part of Walley's make-up. His one chance was to try and crash-land on the golf course on Morden Park. Bill Miles continued:

[Peter] displayed great courage in his moment of danger, he just had to keep his fighter in the air to avoid the built-up area and only when he had succeeded did he think of his own safety. By

Hurricanes of 615 Squadron take
to the air.

Peter's grave, airmen's corner
Whyteleaf cemetery.

then it was too late and his plane had stalled. Morden Park is dotted with trees and has a noticeable slope. It was such a pity that this 20-year old boy's luck should run out so early in his career. The part Peter Walley played that Sunday can only fill one with pride and admiration. In that moment of time these details stand out in my memory; engine running but not flat-out, no fire just a heavy exhaust, seeing daylight through the tail and rudder but not extensive, open cockpit and I'm sure the pilot's left arm was on the left-hand sill, and how dirty the plane looked. I'll never forget that Sunday.

Several other people had witnessed Peter's heroism. The Reverend J.A.G. Ainley, Rector of Morden, was so impressed with the pilot's bravery that he wrote to the Air Ministry as he felt compelled to contact his family to tell them of his unselfish act. Peter's mother later received the Rector's letter:

I am a stranger to you but I am the Rector of this Parish, and I am writing to you in connection with the heroic death of your son Sergeant Peter Walley.

I have been in touch with the Air Ministry and have only just received the necessary information. I want you to know that several people here saw the machine coming down, and they all bear witness to this fact that your son kept to his machine rather than baling out in order that he might prevent it crashing on the houses and so endangering the lives of others. It was wonderful the way he steered it into an open space and so succeeded, but at the cost of his own life.

He was a real hero and gave his life for others, greater love hath no man than this.

At a meeting of the RAOB – Pride of Morden Lodge on Monday 21 August, the Secretary was instructed to write to the Air Force concerning Peter's bravery. His letter, addressed to Sir Archibald Sinclair, Secretary of State for Air, was passed to Peter's mother:

At a meeting of the ... Lodge held on Monday 19 August which was attended by several Brothers resident in the Earl Haig Homes and LCC houses [adjoining] I was instructed to write you, beseeching you to convey, or cause to be conveyed to the next-of-kin, their admiration and pride for the gallant pilot of the aeroplane which crashed on Sunday 18 August at Morden. By what must have been to this gallant airman a superhuman effort, he managed to lift his crashing plane sufficiently to miss by what seemed inches the homes of the men maimed in the last war, and by his action avoided what might have proved to be a terrible calamity.

To the relatives of this gallant pilot, who we feel sure, gave his life in order that we might live, we extend our deepest sympathy and we would like them to know that all brothers on 'The Link' reverently observed two minutes silence on behalf of this gallant soldier and gentleman.

A third letter received by Peter's mother was the hardest to write. It was the letter written by Peter's Commanding Officer, Squadron Leader Joe Kayll. The CO of any operational squadron has often to write such letters but that does not make any of them easier:

It is with great regret that I have to tell you that your son was killed last Sunday.

It is difficult to tell exactly what happened as his section leader was also shot down and is now in hospital wounded. The squadron was at 26,000 feet and we were climbing up to attack the enemy aircraft above us when we were ourselves attacked by Me109 fighters. In the dog-fight that followed your son must have been hit and he crashed on Morden golf course.

Although your son had not been with the squadron very long he succeeded in making himself very popular and was a keen and willing pilot. I had intended to recommend him for a commission as soon as he had got a little more experience.

You have the satisfaction of knowing that he played his part bravely, and I wish to offer my sympathy in the sad times through which you must be passing. If there is anything I can do, please do not hesitate to let me know.

As regards his personal kit, his billet was unfortunately hit by a bomb and nothing has been recovered yet, but if anything is found it will have to be sent to the Central Depot, Cohnbrook, who will communicate with you.

The unveiling of Peter's memorial plaque, Merton Technical College on 13 May 1972. The Mayor of Merton is speaking while Group Captain Cheshire VC looks on. Peter's mother is at Cheshire's right.

The Memorial Plaque.

Peter was buried in the 'Airmen's Corner' in Whyteleaf cemetery just below RAF Kenley, alongside the others who died in the bombing at Kenley on that day.

*

Gradually the years passed, Peter Walley's last flight fading from memory. The war continued; so many were to die before peace was finally won. Peter became little more than a statistic for historians and the like, just one more of the gallant Few to die. Yet he was not totally forgotten by the older residents who remained and continued to live near Morden Park. In the late 1960's plans were agreed to build a new technical college in the Park, close to the exact spot where Peter's Hurricane crashed. Mrs Gertrude Hall wrote to the local newspaper in early 1970 when the site was being prepared. 1970 was of course the thirtieth Anniversary of the Battle of Britain.

RESIDENTS CALL FOR MEMORIAL TO PILOT

A Battle of Britain pilot was shot down and killed on what is now the site of Merton's new technical college. Residents want a plaque put up in his memory.

People stood in their gardens and watched the plane as it burst into flames. Now thirty years later they want to record his bravery ... on the site where he died.

Mrs Hall, Lower Morden Lane, remembers the day vividly: 'We had a clear view across the park and saw him crash. Now they are building on the spot and we think he should be remembered ...' Mrs Hall continued: 'There has been so much said about the Battle of Britain this year and yet nothing is said about this man who obviously saved lives by gliding over our houses. I think young people should be aware of people like him who died for us.'

Gradually over the next few months more details became known and remembered of Peter Walley. The author of this book also responded, writing to both the newspaper and local council who had agreed to commemorate Peter's act. It was finally agreed that a memorial plaque would be placed at the entrance to the new college, the cost being raised by local subscriptions following an appeal by the Mayor of Merton. £300 was needed – £300 was raised.

On Saturday 13 May 1972, at 4pm, the Merton Technical College was officially opened by Group Captain Leonard Cheshire VC DSO DFC, presided over by the Mayor of Merton, Mr J.L. Coombes. Following the opening ceremony, the Group Captain and officials went outside to the entrance. Following a short address by the Mayor and Group Captain Cheshire, and watched by Peter Walley's mother, the Group Captain unveiled the plaque as a Royal Air Force Guard of Honour provided by the RAF Regiment presented arms. In his address the Group Captain recalled Peter Walley's bravery:

> It was not a desperate action – he had plenty of time to jump if he had wanted to. But he remained where he was, thinking of others. He kept his head and kept his skill and so saved others at the expense of his own life. Today this is the best way we can honour him, as we honour other men, whether servicemen or civilians, who did their own bit and paid the price for the rest of the world.

Standing on a table nearby was a scale model of Peter's Hurricane, made in some detail by Bill Miles, the boy who had seen Peter in his moment of decision when he sacrificed his life for others.

THIS PLAQUE HAS BEEN ERECTED BY
PUBLIC SUBSCRIPTION
TO HONOUR THE MEMORY OF
No. 819018 SGT P.K. WALLEY
BATTLE OF BRITAIN PILOT No. 615 SQUADRON R. AUX. A.F.,
WHO WHEN HE WAS 20 YEARS OF AGE WAS KILLED
WHEN HIS HURRICANE CRASHED NEAR THIS SPOT
ON THE 18th AUGUST 1940, HAVING BEEN SHOT
DOWN BY ENEMY RAIDERS.
IT IS RECALLED WITH PRIDE THAT
KNOWING HE WAS ABOUT TO CRASH
SGT WALLEY BRAVELY MANAGED TO GUIDE
HIS BADLY DAMAGED AIRCRAFT OVER NEARBY HOUSES
THEREBY SAFEGUARDING THE LIVES OF THE RESIDENTS.

2

Nigel

When the bloom is off the garden,
And I'm fighting in the sky,
When the lawns and flower beds harden,
And when weak birds starve and die,
The death-roll will grow longer,
Eyes will be moist and red;
And the more I kill, the longer
Shall I miss friends who are dead.

These are the words of Archibald Nigel Charles Weir. With other poems it was found after his death in action and was published in a small book entitled *Verses of a Fighter Pilot* (Faber & Faber Ltd, 1941).

Nigel was born on 2 June 1919. His father Archibald Graham Weir had been in the Royal Flying Corps in the Great War, being captured in 1915. He was exchanged eventually and remained in the RAF until 1925. When Nigel was born, the family was in rented accommodation in Hythe, Kent, but as a small child he was taken to Egypt where his father was serving. When he was three the family returned to England, living at Forest Lodge near Andover, on the edge of Harewood Forest. It had a twelve-acre field running down to the forest where Nigel, with his younger brother and sister and Diana, the eldest of the four, spent much of their time as children, climbing trees and getting to know the wild life of the woodlands and water meadows of the River Test beyond.

Their father also encouraged butterfly and moth breeding and collecting, and he used to take the children out at night with candles in jam jars to attract moths. Nigel became very interested in bird photography although he only possessed an old Brownie camera which required enormous patience. He also liked to draw birds and later enjoyed building model aeroplanes. Not unnaturally, with an ex-RAF squadron leader father and an uncle,

Philip Bartlett, who had won the DSC and bar flying day bombers with the RNAS in WW1, Nigel took a keen interest in flight and flying. This passion took on a greater significance when his father went to Oxford as the founder adjutant of the newly-formed Oxford University Air Squadron. In 1928 Nigel and John were sent to Abberley Hall, Worcester, then went to Winchester College, where Nigel became captain of the fencing team.

He continued with his fencing when he went to Christ Church, Oxford and got his half-blue during his first term. At the outbreak of war he was captain-elect of the University team. He also joined, and became a keen member of the Air Squadron, being granted a commission in the RAFVR in June 1939. During school holidays, he spent time in Switzerland, France and Austria, being able eventually to speak fluent French and German. At Oxford he studied for the Diplomatic Service but decided that he would not enjoy life as a civil servant, and turned his endeavours to medicine. He spent vacations studying in London during which time he did voluntary work in London's poorer districts.

A slight eyesight defect had put a shadow over his flying career but this improved with exercises which enabled him to qualify for the RAF when war came. In the autumn and winter of 1939-40 he attended No 2 Flying Training School at Brize Norton. He had always written regularly to his parents and family, and his letters over the next year give us a wonderful insight into his thoughts during his final training and later active service. His father, by this time, had rejoined the RAF and in 1940 was at Headquarters, Fighter Command.

28 February 1940 (from Brize Norton) : The results of our exam came out yesterday and I managed to be ninth out of forty with 81%, when the top man got 88½% and the second 85%, and I had not less than 70% on any paper, so I can't feel the results were as bad as I feared. Unfortunately the course had five failures – better than other schools, but still a pity. I have done 2½ hours flying now, on low level and high dive bombing, and air to ground and air to air firing – fairly successfully so far. If the weather and organisation would improve I might get some more. Unfortunately the triggers of our guns are so stiff and awkward that by the time the thing finally goes off, the machine is off the aim. It is damned stupid and unnecessary, and we are going to complain until the job is done. Any of us could do it ourselves, if allowed to. As the trigger operates through a Bowden cable, it would be better to simply pull up a ring at the side somewhere instead of pushing a stiff lever through an inch and a half on a sensitive control column! Until further notice (owing to mud) we are not retracting wheels, for when we recommenced flying three days ago, we had six if not seven crashes – and only one by a pupil! I'm not surprised some of the staff pilots crash; thank God we only have a little dual.

Then came a posting to an Operational Training Unit (OTU), still at Brize Norton. Just after Easter 1940 he wrote to his mother:

> ... I have got leave for Sunday and Monday. Unfortunately that does not prevent them from putting me on night-flying to-night at 2.30 am and if I am to reach London before tea-time I have to catch a seven o'clock train from here tomorrow morning, which looks as if it will shorten the weekend I need *badly* ... It is good to hear that Diana has some leave, I expect she needs it. I have a feeling that in view of numerous week-ends, Christmas leave is likely to prove my last bit of leave for some time. The weather here has been foul, and flights few and far between – but what we do is fun. Our Harvard flight is apparently considered a bit exceptional, and early on they taught us to fly formation overlapped, which is fun, especially on dives and zooms. Nevertheless we are not up to programme, which is disheartening, for we could have been, easily. On 8 April we go to Penrhos, North Wales. It should be quite fun using live rounds for a change. Till then we remain here as senior course on the station, counting the days and wondering where our postings will take us. I hope it will be on the main line between London and Salisbury, so as to enable me to see something of the family in odd off-moments ...

On 18 April he wrote to his father from Penhros, Pwllheli, North Wales:

> ... Hurried line to give you some of the results so far. The firing takes place at 230 yards (harmonisation point) and the bombing

is done by instinct for we have no bomb sights and the target is out of sight under the nose when the bomb is released ... On quarter attacks most of us have only fired once. Only three people have hit the drogue – each with one bullet out of 100 (which is five seconds firing). It is most improbable that we shall get any more air to air firing, and my puny average of $4\frac{1}{2}\%$ is third at present! On the bombing I have best average and individual score.

On the same date he wrote a long letter to his mother and included:

I seem to be an ace bomber and only an average shot so far, which is a pity. In the evenings we sometimes go out to neighbouring villages for dinner and a drink. Yesterday while waiting my turn on the target I found a deep cleft about forty yards wide between two enormous towering masses of cumulus. I went through it and when I came round to try again I found the slipstream had turned it into a long tunnel like a rabbit-hole, so I went through again, and try the same thing again now whenever I find nice cloud ravines. The flight up here was grand too, for we went skimming low in formation over the surf and up just over the hill tops.

Another letter to his father shortly after revealed:

This is a very good spot and in so far as the serviceability of aircraft permits we are getting some good practice (unfortunately in training aircraft the standard of serviceability is appalling, as they are maintained by conscripts and reservists for the most part, and in any case spares seem almost unobtainable.) Fortunately we have a few picked airmen with us, and they work like mad, so that when five aircraft go wrong – say two for gun air pressure, two with sights gone wrong and one with a bent wing tip – they take the two worst and take from them the necessary wing tip, pressure bottles or sights to repair the remaining three. Someone has opened a book on the results – the best individual result in each exercise winning that particular race. It applied to low level bombing, air to air firing and air to ground firing. Unfortunately I have not been able to get more than 4-1 odds on

Nigel Weir

myself for anything, as I have started off rather well. Our gun in
the Harvard is harmonised to coincide with the line of sight at
230 yards. If you fire at a range of 50 yards too near or too far,
with the sights dead on, you are bound to miss; so it's a bit
tricky, more especially as a little red cone three foot across is not
the easiest object on which to gauge range. Even then you may
have sights that vibrate or else are too dim to see properly, or oil
spattering the windscreen. The result is that only one person has
hit the cone so far – and he was not specially bright in the air to
ground stuff. Anyway, no instructor has hit it yet!

Completing his training and having received his pilot's 'wings',
Nigel was posted to 504 Squadron based at RAF Tangmere on the
south coast. Here he added flying time to his log, went onto
Hurricane fighters but changed squadrons just as the 'balloon went
up!' in France at dawn on 10 May 1940. In this his father was able
to pull a few strings. Had Nigel known that 504 Squadron was
about to go to the war in France, one wonders if he would have
been so keen to change units. The day before the Germans invaded
the Lowlands, Nigel Weir wrote to his father at HQ Fighter
Command:

I have completed the necessary three hours on a Magister and
yesterday went solo – not that there's any other way – on a
Hurricane. The cockpit layout is a terrible tangle but I contrived
to memorise the formidable sequence of action necessary to effect
a circuit and get round safely, in fact very stylishly, without
dipping as I got the wheels up. On the second landing, however,
I came in rather fast and floated in completely still air just above
the ground. There is no 'feel' to tell you when to stall her, and
finally I tentatively eased the stick back and increased the
incidence. The machine ballooned up to about three feet and
stalled and the starboard wing sunk with a horrible wallowing
feeling. It ever so nearly touched the ground but I crashed on
opposite rudder and got down safely. I did three or four more
landings, all very good, and then came in. The flight commander
had touched a wing tip that morning and a fellow pilot tells me
that when his squadron got Hurricanes they stuffed in eight
wings in the first week – all on calm days. So I'm glad to have

learnt without mishap. In future I shall come down steeper and slower and not float so far.

And the next day he wrote:

> I have heard that 145 Squadron is coming here very soon ... that it is VP (variable pitch) airscrew Hurricanes such as I have flown ... feel it might be a good thing to try and get posted to it – especially if there is a chance of getting to France soon.

This letter and hint worked for the very next day, 11 May, he heard from his father who had evidently arranged for the necessary posting:

> Thank you very much indeed for taking so much trouble for me. As a result I have been posted to 145 and thus remain here. They seem quite a nice crowd but if, after a month or two, I can get back to my squadron in France or join Michael Peacock[1], should he be given a squadron, I should be only too pleased. I was duty pilot last night, and what with the moves, arrivals and departures, X-raids – friendly bombers lost – I hardly sat down all night.

No 504 Squadron, along with 3 and 79, was sent to re-inforce the Air Component on 10 May. Nigel arrived on 145 Squadron on the 12th. 145 was at Tangmere so it only meant changing squadrons, not aerodromes. On the 15th he wrote again to his father:

> I am very well off here, as I share a room with another pilot in the same position as me; we have both done ten hours on Hurricanes and go up with the flight commander together. The last news I heard of 504 (Squadron) was Percy and two others I knew well killed in the Bombay, and the other friends I had in it smashed up. Two pilots killed in action and one missing – all exceptionally nice fellows and most of these married. Mrs Percy is about to have a baby. Against this 38 Huns down in three or

---

[1] Peacock was in 601 Squadron and shortly afterwards commanded 85 Squadron but was killed in action soon afterwards.

four days. Still, if I had gone, I should have gone in the Bombay –
so I'm not sorry.

So apparently he had a narrow escape by not remaining with 504.
There was also some speculation that 145 Squadron might be sent
to France as indicated to his mother on 18 May. The main part of
the letter concerned the occasion of his approaching 21st birthday
but continued:

> ... but still, with the Germans halfway to Paris, I may have to go
> before the end of the month! ... I'm afraid they will guard
> against having a second battle of the Marne sprung on them, and
> it sounds hard to stop their tanks if the latter, as soon as they
> meet anti-tank positions, merely take cover and wireless back for
> dive bombers to come and dislodge the defence. However, let us
> hope for the best and not be shaken by the worst.

As it turned out, the squadron did not go to France. Instead the
RAF in France had mostly to evacuate. Only units of the Advanced
Air Striking Force continued to operate to the south-west of Paris.
Further north the Dunkirk evacuation began at the end of May and
145 and Nigel Weir were involved in that.

Most mornings, 145 would fly along to Lympne, refuel and be
ready for operations over the evacuation beaches. On the 28th
Nigel wrote about his squadron's activities and his own theories on
the fighting to come:

> I'm getting on fine here and what ciné results I have are 100%
> hits and ranged right too. I imagine we shall be fighting the
> world's bloodiest rear guard action in a day or two when the
> Allies clear out and embark to leave NE France and Belgium.
> There will be swarms of bombers and fighters attacking troop
> ships and I suppose naval guns will have to try and hold back the
> German troops for a day or so. A lot of hope they've got! I was
> infuriated again to see in the papers yesterday evening or hear in
> the news that the latest Air Ministry communiqué said the RAF
> had shot down thirty enemy aircraft and five of our aircraft are
> missing. In 145 alone, nine went out and three came back. 601
> had two missing and I knew of twelve others missing in three

squadrons. Two of our fellows were definitely shot down in flames – dead – making five of our boys definitely dead in a week and others missing. But a number of 110s were floating on the water when 145 had done with them. I'm due to go over any day now. As they will probably lose all but half a dozen operational pilots, I may go tomorrow – armed with a certain knowledge of how other lads were done in.

I have my theories about this fighting against greater numbers of machines, some of which are far superior in performance. Assuming the AA don't get one and several of our boys were brought down by Hun AA which seems incredibly accurate – height would seem our best weapon; one can attack at very high speed, abeam for bomber formations, as their cross fire has killed those who tried from behind and then climb up in the most erratic and manoeuvring way possible, with one's eyes skinned. If there are too many on top of you and you don't have much ammunition after the first attack – cut the dog-fight and get home. One can always reload at Hawkinge and come back with a lot of height and it's better than losing one of our only too scarce fighters for nothing. And if the new Heinkels chase you[1], well, its just too bad! One can always bale out and swim home!

I have been practising jerky unsteady turns, and pulling the sights off the mark and getting them back quickly. I think it will pay in the end, more than thousands of Fighter Command attacks – which are all very fine if you just meet three bombers in a clear sky and they hold formation and fly along like gents. But to have to fly in formation and follow a set method is suicide now; one just has to fling the thing about and watch below and above and behind and in front all at once. I'd like to see the people who send us round orders on how to attack formations of fighters come and show us how when we only have a few and they have swarms above and below! I shall fight with the aim of getting the maximum number of Huns during the period when their destruction is most vital – and not at being a bloody fool.

A friend of mine – he hit the sea in flames yesterday – shot

---

[1] Referring to the Heinkel 113 fighter which everyone thought was about to come to the front. It was, however, purely a propaganda aeroplane and did not see action in spite of many pilots reporting them in combat.

dead before he opened fire on the winger of a bomber formation –
landed at Dieppe a few days ago to refuel. As soon as he landed
dive-bombers came over and he then saw that some of the young
RAF men and officers were already raving mad. He dived into a
ditch and a couple of women and a lot of children were machine-
gunned dead beside him before they reached cover. He managed
to fill up from cans and go up and get one, but everyone there
among the wreckage, everyone begged him to stay and defend
their aerodrome overnight. Another lad came down on the wrong
side, dropped in (by parachute) to a pub, had a couple of drinks,
and was then told his error, so he ran three miles and swam a
canal and got back after arrest as a fifth columnist. He called in
at an aerodrome where twelve Hurricanes had been destroyed
and others damaged on the first dive of some raiding (Ju) 87s.
One squadron had had three CO's in a week, and two others
counted five survivors – though some were probably only
missing.

Lots of fellows get back to this mess after several days, having
had a few odd experiences. So one way and another, though one
inevitably loses many good friends, life is interesting and may
soon provide a good bit of fun. There's only one thing I really
pray to be spared and that is to be shot as a parachutist!

On 1 June Nigel Weir had his first successful taste of action. At 5.35
am nine Hurricanes flew along to Lympne where they joined
aircraft to form a composite wing formation over Dunkirk but no
enemy aircraft were encountered. They landed back at Manston
from where they took off at 11 am when enemy aircraft were
reported north of Dunkirk. The British formation consisted of 39
aircraft of which 12 were French Bloch 152s.

Near Dunkirk they sighted large formations of German
aeroplanes – estimated to be seventy in number. Messerschmitt 110s
flying at 6,000 feet, Messerschmitt 109s above. Weir was leading a
section under his flight commander, Flight Lieutenant A.H. Boyd
who had already destroyed at least four German planes over
Dunkirk during the evacuation. As the Hurricane pilots of 145, in a
position north of the enemy and flying eastwards, looked towards
the German formation they saw below them about thirty Me110s.

Nigel Weir's section dived on them and he attacked the rear

machine but before he got his sights on the 110s formed a defensive circle finding himself a part of that circle. He was, however, quite happy for a few seconds for the packed formation prevented them firing at him. He turned to cut across the circle, one Me110 opening fire at him with the rear-gun, and as he ducked instinctively, another 110 came into his sights. He opened fire on a beam attack from sixty yards and blew the German machine's nose off, also part of its port engine. The 110 stood up on its tail and Boyd watched it fall away and crash into the sea, confirming Weir's first victory.

Weir dived, then climbed meeting an Me109. He pulled his Hurricane into a very steep climb and gave it a short burst from 200 yards right into its belly. He saw his tracer shells enter the 109's fuselage and it ceased to climb and began to go down. Then bullets began to pass him so he quickly kicked the rudder and skidded away before going into a spin. Pulling out at 1,000 feet, he regained height over the sea but the enemy were fast disappearing into France, so, joining up with Boyd, they flew home.

Back at base, Weir, who had been flying Hurricane P2951, was credited with one Me110 destroyed plus the 109 as probably destroyed. Boyd had shot down a 110 and a 109. Roy Dutton, A flight commander, had also got a 110 and two 109s. Pilot Officers R.D. Yule and M.A. Newling each claimed 110s. The squadron lost one pilot and another was shot up but got back to Manston. Apparently both Dutton and Weir were attacked by 'friendly' Hurricanes but they were not hit.

Weir flew several more patrols over the final stages of the withdrawal from France but had no further successes. On 17 June he wrote an extremely interesting letter to his father. The first part recorded here, was, for someone so young, strangely prophetic. His later reference to Fifth Column was something everyone was mindful of at this period of the war. Everyone was, not unnaturally, very jumpy and many innocent occurrences grew out of all proportion in consequence.

> ... If the Huns get the French fleet we are outnumbered in every class of ship but aircraft carriers. If we lose the French Air Force we have but a fraction of their numbers and French colonies are opposite Gib and Aden. But still, our great asset seems to be that once free from liabilities in France, we can concentrate all on

Home Defence and begin playing for time. Oil is against them (unless the whole German Army goes to the Middle East) and one day the Empire and American air effort will tell – and once we clear them from the skies they are at our mercy. But we look like having some nasty moments before then, especially when one thinks what they have achieved through force and Fifth Column against the land and air forces of half Europe in the last month.

Talking of Fifth Column, we were at Warmwell yesterday and before leaving were warned to check our petrol and run up our motors very carefully as they had seventeen crashes in a month – killing nine – due to tanks having been drained of all but five minutes petrol and to water having been added. We got out all right, except that three people had their radios effectively dealt with. If I see any windows lit up at night after a warning of raids, I shall shoot at it. Pattern signals on the ground seem to have done enough harm in France, including they say, the sudden appearance of an avenue of lighted windows leading to the hotel in which GHQ was, about a minute before it was bombed! But these hot nights people draw back their curtains and then, as soon as sirens go, reach for the switch.

This letter was followed by another dated 27 June:

I get five days' leave dating from Monday, on which day I will come up to town. I hope you are getting slightly lighter work in this period between blitz and blitz, for everyone looks like having a heavy job when it starts. As you know, Max Aitken got one last night which was a good show. I'm glad we have one to the station's credit at last, for we should have had two sitters already but for Ops: and, on one occasion, searchlights also.

The reference to Max Aitken refers to the night of 26 June when Aitken, CO of No 601 Squadron, destroyed a Heinkel 111 at night flying from Tangmere.

*

Early July and the opening phase of the Battle of Britain began, the dangerous and costly battles over the Channel convoys and coastal ports. 145, right on the south coast, was in the forefront of these early battles. On 11 July, the squadron's CO, Squadron Leader J.R.A. Peel, was shot down in the late afternoon but was rescued by the Selsey lifeboat. The previous day, following a spot of leave, Weir wrote:

> I'm afraid I was not with the squadron on the show you mention, but we have been very busy ever since then. Unfortunately Blue Section have not yet made an interception – entirely thanks to the sector controllers – but we have been very cold for hours on end at 28,000 feet and had very little sleep – as we're generally off on the first flap well before 4 am and usually get dragged in to do someone's job till nearly midnight. So at least we feel we're trying and it is great fun because there is a conttinual prospect of meeting Huns. I wouldn't miss a flight for anything and shall stay on on my release days for the most part, as one cannot get far enough afield to make good use of them. I also heard that your idea of mobile pillboxes had been thought a good idea by the War Office.

The battles over the Channel were hotting up as July progressed. On the 18th elements of 145 Squadron were scrambled ten times but only one contact was made with the Luftwaffe. Shortly before 1 pm, B Flight was ordered to patrol base at 10,000 feet, Boyd leading (in P3381), with Pilot Officer P.W. Dunning-White (P3896), Weir (P2918), and Pilot Officers P.L. Parrott, D.N. Forde and J.E. Storrar.

Shortly after take-off they were ordered to fly course 240° and in order to see any hostile aircraft against the cloud layer, climbed to 12,000 feet. Weir, flying as Blue 2, saw an aircraft flying south over the sea, two thousand feet below. Boyd was having trouble with his radio, Weir being unable to raise him and even the Controller was unable to make contact, therefore, Weir took the lead and dived. Boyd followed and when Weir was nearly in range, he pulled to the right to allow Boyd to open fire. Weir opened fire simultaneously from the quarter, closing to astern when Boyd broke away. Boyd in fact, had been hit by return fire from the German's rear gunner.

It was a Heinkel 111 and Weir followed it into some thin cloud, the German pilot taking violent evasive action. Several large panels or pieces of the aircraft broke from the Heinkel, forcing Weir to break away.

The other three Hurricanes, Green Section, took over the attack and the bomber went into the sea twenty miles south of Bognor Regis at 1.15 pm, one crewman being seen in the water. This Heinkel, of Stab/KG27, was flown by the *Geschwader Kommandeur*, Oberst Georgi.

Four days later came further success for Blue Section when at 6.20 am, they were ordered to patrol Beachy Head to Selsey Bill when enemy aircraft were reported. Just before 7 o'clock Weir spotted one some distance away, flying south but Boyd (P3381) had seen a Dornier 17 below at 15,000 feet and dived. Green Section was left behind but Blue Section dived flat-out as the bomber dived east. Boyd's fire silenced the rear gunner and damaged the starboard engine. As soon as he broke away, Weir (P2981) opened fire from above at 300 yards' range, aiming ahead of the cockpit. With no visible effect he transferred his fire to the starboard engine which caught fire. Dunning-White (P2720) then attacked and the Dornier finally belly-landed on the sea, twenty miles south of Selsey. Boyd signalled a motor boat to rescue the crew and then turned for base. Weir had fired 330 rounds from each of his guns. The Dornier was from 4(F)/121, piloted by Leutnant Borman. On the 22nd he wrote again to his father:

Yesterday we were patrolling over some shipping (6 of us) when about 50 Hun fighters and bombers arrived. They hesitated, and we got reinforced by driblets – finally they went off home without dropping bombs. I chased an Me109 which tried to join in and pretend to be a Hurricane, but I could not catch it. This story is incomplete; the rest of it is so incredible and reflects so badly on some senior people that I will not write it down on paper. This morning Blue Section found a Dornier 17, and Boyd as usual silenced the rear guns at some cost to his own aircraft. He also damaged the starboard engine. I followed from above, aiming ahead of the pilot, and as that had no effect I put the rest of my ammunition into the starboard engine and it began to flame. Blue 3 finished it off, and I went off and morsed to a Norwegian motor torpedo boat to come and collect the Hun; as Blue 3 could not morse he was unable to do much in this line. As with the Heinkel, there was only one left alive in the water; this one however was lucky enough to be rescued. We are hoping that soon a fair number of us will run into a real bunch of Huns who will stay and fight. They don't seem very keen on meeting us at the moment.

*

As August began (the squadron having moved to Tangmere's satellite airfield at Westhampnett) so too came the main assault by the Luftwaffe. On Thursday the 8th, 145 Squadron was heavily engaged and Nigel Weir had his most successful day.

The main battle that day centred above and around a coastal Channel convoy known as Convoy CW9 – code-named PEEWIT. It had sailed from the Medway on the evening of the 7th. German radar picked up the ships and an E-boat attack at dawn sank three of the vessels. As daylight came, an all-out air assault was launched by the dive-bombing Ju87s, escorted by fighters. Several RAF squadrons were scrambled to defend PEEWIT, 145 being one.

Again flying P2918, Weir took-off with Boyd (P3221) and B Flight at 8.45 am to reinforce A Flight already above the convoy, when many 'bandits' were reported approaching. About one minute before B Flight arrived, A Flight engaged fighters and when Boyd and his boys came onto the scene just south of the Needles at 12,000 feet, waves of bombers swept by. Green Section went after them and so did Boyd but it all happened so quickly that Weir was left behind in the turn. As he dived after the others, three Me109s crossed in front of him and one peeled off onto the tail of Blue 3. Weir charged at the Messerschmitt, fired and followed as the 109 dived. It began to leave a trail of smoke and continuing down dived straight into the sea.

As he pulled up, the sky seemed clear of all aircraft, but then he saw a second wave of Stukas passing on his right. Joining up with another Hurricane, Weir attacked from astern, firing into nine or ten Ju87s. Crossing right behind one he closed to within twenty yards and gave it a burst from below. White smoke immediately trailed back as Weir broke away. Following his victim he saw the Stuka drop its bombs over the ships but they fell well wide. Closing

(Right) Nigel and his father watching some aircraft. Photo taken on Nigel's last leave, September, 1940.

(Below) A group of 145 Squadron pilots study a German Mae West. Nigel is sitting second from the right. Tangmere, 1940.

again he hammered the bomber again and it crashed into the sea. Flying with Green 3 he attacked and chased another Ju87 using up his remaining ammunition but to no avail. He landed back at base at 9.30.

One-four-five Squadron had lost two pilots killed in this, the first of three fights it fought on the 8th, but had claimed several victories. Further success came in a second scrap with Ju87s at 12.30 pm and then a further fight developed south of the Isle of Wight when more claims were made although Me110s shot down three more pilots from the squadron.

Nigel Weir gained his third victory of the day during this second battle. 145 became airborne at 11.50 and headed south of the Isle of Wight where enemy aircraft were reported. High above he saw what he thought were 26 He111s and Me110s but most likely they were all 110 fighters. Being unable to engage these they returned to Dungeness and were then vectored towards the convoy. Flying west towards the IoW area they then turned south to cut off any retreating hostile aircraft. They saw some Me110s in two groups at 2,000 feet with 109s at 7,000 feet. Three Hurricanes could be seen circling at 12,000 feet probably wondering how best to attack and requesting assistance. A few minutes later when about to dive, an Me109 flew across in front of Weir's Hurricane (P2918), Weir believing it to be a decoy. Nevertheless he pulled round after it, got onto its tail and flew round in circles with it. Just as he was gaining a favourable position on its tail the 109 pilot dived steeply but Weir fired from behind at 500 yards. He had to pull out to attack some 110s but Boyd saw the 109 go into the sea. Weir fired at two 110s but made no claims.

Three victories for Weir, of a total of 21 claimed by the squadron, won for him the Distinguished Flying Cross. He had now been involved in the destruction of six German aircraft plus one probably destroyed.

*

One-four-five was again in action on the 11th and 12 August but suffered more casualties. Two pilots were lost on the 11th, and Squadron Leader Peel was wounded. Nigel Weir himself was a casualty on the 11th, flying P2918. He had scrambled at 9.50 am and shortly after 10 am, 145 became embroiled with German fighters. Over the Isle of Wight, Swanage and Portland many combats took place by several RAF squadrons. Weir, hit by fire from a fighter, was forced to crash-land near Christchurch, fortunately without serious injury except that his Hurricane was a write-off. Losing three further pilots on the 12th despite inflicting casualties on the enemy, 145 Squadron, having lost ten pilots in five days had to be pulled out of the battle. They flew north to Drem in Scotland to reform. From here Weir wrote to his brother John on the 21st:

> Among our new pilots we have one or two brilliant ones; two have Huns to their credit already, one three or four and the other 17. They also cope easily with formation rolls and so forth. 90% of them have seen action already which is a great help. This seems a quiet spot with plenty of grouse shooting and fishing to be had for the asking. The food is the best I have yet met in the Air Force, so that altogether this is a much better place than I expected. Given good weather and a few Huns it would be perfect. Nevertheless we are all longing to get back to 11 Group. A little more sun and Hun would do us all good. If we can manage it − and I know they want us back − I shall be a little nearer home. Apparently local families hearing that a war-worn squadron had come to recuperate, had all clamoured to give them hospitality. These people were surprised to find their guests were not all hysterical wrecks, but once they had tumbled to this the chaps all had riding and shooting and fishing to their hearts' content!

On 31 August the award of Nigel's DFC was announced. Congratulatory letters were received, one from his former house-master at Winchester College to which he replied:

> As well you know, I am not the sort to earn any decoration and it was only given to me because the dozen or so magnificent fellows who had deserved several times over more than I can ever deserve, chanced to be of the many who take-off and never return. I personally have great respect for the wily Hun, having been outwitted and shot down by him once already; and although these periods of idleness make us all eager to get back

down south, I know that next time I see squadrons of Huns circling round high above, and waiting for us to attack them, I shall be just as terrified as on previous occasions, and just as thankful when it is all over. One day I suppose I shall have to lead others in these things. I pray the day is still far off, for I have survived by watching, following and copying an exceptionally brilliant Flight Commander[1]. The thought of having others as dependent on me as I am on him is quite appalling!

Following the hectic days in the south, the rest in Scotland was more than welcome but soon the comparative inactivity became a bore. In between training new pilots, 145 Squadron was moved to RAF Dyce, near Aberdeen. From here Weir wrote to his father on 17 September:

I have just finished 48 hours readiness followed by 24 hours readiness and 15 minutes available mixed, and have now had a bath and a shave and feel better. Not having a maintenance flight here we are having some trouble with serviceability, but are just scraping along. We have just got a new Intelligence Officer who saw you at HQ and brought cheerful messages which were very welcome. Since we have been here two Huns have received short bursts from us, but the weather is so foul that they have both escaped into the cloud at once. However, the weather is so awful that a Heinkel came down last night through weather alone! I have done a lot of section leading since I have been here and the odd night sortie as well – but night sorties in this weather give small hope of interception.

Then the following day, news pertaining to the future of 145 Squadron having percolated through, he wrote to his father:

I have heard that pilots from 145 are to be taken and drafted to squadrons in the south as replacements; that AOC 14 Group is trying to get Boyd the squadron, if any trying should be needed, and that we shall be left with him, two flight commanders, two

[1] Adrian Hope Boyd, later Group Captain DSO DFC* – he survived the war.

section leaders and perhaps the odd pilot. The rest to be filled in and trained up. In case you should wonder what I should like my fate to be, I should like to stay with the squadron rather than anything else, come what may of it.

A short time later Adrian Boyd was in fact given command of the squadron. Nigel was still receiving letters of congratulations from various people and when Flight Lieutenant R.F. Boyd of 602 Squadron received a DFC, Nigel's mother confused the two names. As can be seen, his mother too was doing her bit for the war effort. He wrote to her on 24 September:

It must have been another Boyd who got the DFC. Ours has now got the squadron which is grand! You seem to be very busy with your guard duty, which must be cold work now. We are fairly busy too and I have had as much as three days on at a stretch, all readiness. One does not feel very clean after three days and nights in one's clothes. I have already written twenty-eight answers to congratulation letters and have fourteen more to do.

Meanwhile his father seems to have pulled certain strings at Fighter Command HQ as is confirmed in a letter Nigel wrote to him on 5 October:

Thank you for safeguarding my position in 145. As a matter of fact we have lost four – two original members, one who joined with me, and the section leader of yellow section. We have apparently got to lose two more to reduce us to sixteen but they are neither of them me. We had a fairly uneventful trip up from Hatfield, though much of it, including the take-off, was blind. I don't know much about it as I read 150 pages of a book on the way up. The other night one of our Belgians was on patrol over a convoy (convoys have about four ships a week sunk by bombs at night round us!) – a patrol we do on every convoy as the Blenheims say they are not night operational and refused the job. This time however, they sent three over without bothering to phone across the aerodrome to tell us, and we knew nothing about it. The convoy was bombed and its AA opened up, but ceased fire to let our chap shoot a Heinkel down. He then saw another twin loom up in front and in a second burst before it fired the recognition lights he put twenty bullets in it, shooting down the undercarriage. Fortunately no one was hurt in the crash-landing it made later.

The Blenheim had the face to claim the Hun and the AM Communique credited them with it, though they are the sole witnesses, whereas the District Intelligence Officer, the convoy's AA gunners and the Heinkel crew all of whom witnessed the whole thing, credit it to our chap, as does the Blenheim rear gunner, who says they only attacked it as it was crashing (tail shot away!) A bit hard, as it is this lad's first chance at a Hun. I suppose there is no chance of our going to Liverpool where there seem to be a few Hun bombers all day long. P.S. My investiture is on 15.10.40, 10.15 am. I am getting two tickets allowed for friends and relatives.

The Belgian pilot was Baudouin de Hemptine who had joined the squadron on 20 August, one of several new pilots and one of three Belgians to be posted in, the other two being Jean Offenberg and Alexis Jottard. The date of the action was 2 October. However, records now show that de Hemptine was later credited with the victory, a Heinkel 115 seaplane from the 1st Staffel, Kustenflieger-gruppe 506.

Then came the news everyone had been waiting for; 145 was to return to the south – back to RAF Tangmere. They flew south on 8 October.

*

The battles in the south had changed considerably since early August. In many people's view the battle had been won, although the Luftwaffe continued to raid southern England. However, with the ending of the summer, the enemy's tactics had changed, the main raids being made by bomb-carrying Me110s and Me109s. It was, in consequence, a most dangerous time for Britain's fighter pilots (not that they had had an easy summer) for the enemy was elusive, often high up and with other fighters just waiting for an opportunity to pounce on the hard climbing Spitfires and Hurricanes. And unencumbered with lumbering bombers to escort as they had had in the previous months, the Messerschmitt pilots were more free to mix it. Amidst the clouds and the autumn glare from the watery sun, death lurked high over the English coast and Channel. Nigel Weir was now flying P2683 as his personal machine. He wrote to his brother from Tangmere on 17 October:

Since we have been here we have not been in for much. Two of our chaps got a recco: seaplane and A Flight got attacked by 109s, losing one killed and one full of bullets and shell splinters (but going to pull through), and getting two. Also on a day I was off two 109s attacked the squadron and shot down one – wounded – while Boyd got the offender as he made off. The trouble is they are always miles above where the sun is very bright, and they dive from the south – so that tracer and cannon shells are the first we know of it. I try to avoid action with the high fighter patrols, for they are harmless as regards ground damage and are only there to get you to fight while they have all the advantages. It is a waste of fighters to engage them but equally you have to go and see what they are, in case they should be bombers; and by that time you have probably been suddenly attacked. God, how we love cloudy days when we can sit undazzled in the cloud base and try to lure them down – but they rarely come in such weather.

On the same day he also wrote to his father:

It is good to be back here at last. Unfortunately there seems to be nothing but 109s and 110s about and the interception apparatus, having been bombed, is awful. We generally get told to patrol 15,000 feet below the Huns, who dive from the south straight out of the sun. Not having polarised goggles, we cannot see them though we do what we can with dark glasses. Also, whatever we are told, we climb as high as we can, preferably inland first and then out to meet what are obviously fighters, though one has to go and make sure they are not bombers. I see no point in engaging 109s at 30,000 feet as they can do no harm up there and when I lead the flight, or the squadron as I have once, I try to keep out of these useless scraps. Flight have unfortunately been engaged twice, with the loss of one killed one very badly wounded and one with flesh wounds only, also two other kites shot to hell.

I have not yet fired my guns and intend to refrain from chasing after decoys and use my guns to protect any of the new fellows who get in a mess. They are all making the mistakes of getting isolated and not realising that Hun fighters work in pairs, even if you can only see one. God knows they've been told often enough. Boyd and one of the new pilots got an Arado Monoplane floatplane and Boyd a 109 as well. Two A Flight boys have also bagged a 109 apiece but it looks as if most of the Hun aircraft must have moved to the Balkans. Anyway the main thing is to save pilots until you can put them in a more modern aeroplane, and as long as I have any say in the matter I shall try to discourage firebrands from attacking harmless offensive patrols that are both more numerous and far better placed than ourselves, and where *raison d'être* is to be attacked in such circumstances, Tangmere is certainly more transparent than when we left!

The actions referred to in these two letters occurred on 12 October when Boyd and Pilot Officer Dudley Honor shot down an Arado 196 floatplane. The two casualties were Sergeant J.V. Wadham and Sergeant Thorpe, shot down by Me109s near Cranbrook, the former being killed, the latter wounded. Three days later Boyd shot down a 109 from JG2 over Christchurch Bay at 12.30 pm but Pilot Officer J Machacek (V7337) was badly wounded by another and had to bale out.

In the book *Lonely Warrior*, the diary of Jean Offenberg, edited by Victor Houart (Souvenir Press, 1956), Offenberg recorded in his diary at this time that Weir was a great clown on occasions and on one occasion made a little speech on aircraft and fighting in his best Oxford accent:

The task of the warrior has always been the same, it is the systematic extermination of the infidel. Today new methods and effective weapons have been put at the disposal of the enthusiasts of this interesting little sport. Among these I must mention that the fighter plane is unrivalled. However, this instrument is not perfect and there are certain things which it refuses to do, namely, (a) to look behind so that it is not shot down stupidly, (b) to place itself at a point exactly 200 yards from the nearest

Nazi airman, (c) to make the necessary firing corrections, and (d) to fire the machine guns. On account of these imperfections for which I blame the scientists, His Majesty's Government has seen fit to engage the services of a certain number of gentlemen like you and I to carry out missions in order to rectify the four points I have just quoted ...

On this occasion the arrival of the truck in which Weir was talking, arrived at the mess, this ending the lesson being given by 'Professor Nigel Weir, professional fighter pilot'.

*

On 23 October Nigel wrote his last letter to his mother:

You seem to have had a most hectic time in London, and all for nothing. I only got the postponement notice [postponing his investiture] the day before, myself. I hope to get five days' leave to coincide with John's leave early next month. It would be a break for him as life must be very dull at Caterham apart from bombs. I had the good fortune to meet two fellows who were in 43 Course with me at Brize Norton. One of them got badly shot up two or three months ago and I found I escorted him back over the Channel! Things are quiet here now and I have not fired my guns. We have only lost one killed and two wounded in over a fortnight – and they were all raw, being in action for the first time. So I don't think you need worry – especially as cloud cover is becoming more general every day.

    Love to you all
    Nigel.
    P.S. I am flying up for a wedding of an FTS friend on Saturday and hope to meet others there.

Five days later he wrote to his father.

I'm afraid the polarised goggles, like all Air Force equipment, is a thing found in orders and reports and even heard of in stores, but quite unprocurable in fact. We continue to lose pilots; one of our Czechs was shot down by a 109 with British rudder markings; he only realised what it was too late. He is in hospital

– our third casualty. The first was killed and the second very badly wounded. Then we had one of our most experienced pilots shot down and wounded by a Hun while he was turning to show his roundels to two Spitfires who attacked him. Yesterday we lost our liveliest and most wide-awake pilot – a little Belgian – and two more shot down in the sea. I have talked with those who survived their shooting down, and it is always the same story – weaving and keeping their eyes skinned for the reported Huns, and then feeling bullets coming from God knows where.

As I climbed to attack some He113s [sic] yesterday (they were 10,000 feet above the height given and as much above the AA bursts, and coming round behind our leader) I looked hard in the sun, knowing my section would be busy trying to hold me in a climbing turn at 25,000 feet, and suddenly saw two diving at us. I only saw them because they got so close that they half obscured the sun! I jammed into a spin and thank God one of my section followed me. The other was looking the other way at the time and they must have just gone behind him.

Anyway, what is getting us down is 11 Group 'P' Staff. They have posted us one or two dud pilots – including one who cannot cloud fly and has consequently been pushed from squadron to squadron for some time. We grounded him, but still after a fortnight cannot get a replacement – only forms and forms to fill in. Also we have applied for replacements for three or four others – wounded or killed or posted sick – and some of them a fortnight ago. We have had no replacements and today, owing to one or two being unfit for a day or two, we could only fly ten. Boyd feels they might post us someone soon, and not all the duffest sergeant pilots they have got. We only have fifteen flying pilots at present and when two or three are shot down and cannot get back for a day or so, it becomes hard to fly a complete squadron. Sorry to put up such a moan, but Boyd asked if perhaps you could chase them.

The experienced pilot referred to in this letter was Pilot Officer R.D. Yule, flying P3926. He saw enemy aircraft below him but someone had left his R/T switched on and he was unable to contact the others. Therefore, he dived, being joined by two Spitfires but he was then fired at by one of the ever elusive 109s and hit in the leg.

His glycol tank was also shot through and he was forced down at Burwash and taken to Penbury Hospital. Although it was first thought that it had been one of the Spitfires who had fired at him, the bullet, when extracted from his leg, proved to be of German origin. This was 23 October.

On the 27th they lost Alexis Jottard, referred to as 'our liveliest and most wide awake pilot' by Weir. He and Pilot Officer F. Weber (Czech) and Sergeant J.K. Haine were all shot down by 109s at 5.15 pm off the Isle of Wight but only Jottard died. On the 31st another letter to his father:

> I was in the Portsmouth barrage one night last week, when the controller mistook me for another aircraft and gave me his vectors. When about fifty searchlights shot up I saw what had happened and cleared out for I was only at 5,000 feet. I also caused an alarm at Winchester and got searchlights (ineffective) and very close blind AA shell, which made the aircraft shake a bit. Mist then closed in and the three of us who were flying spent three-quarters of an hour trying to find the aerodrome; and having done so, trying to find the flare path. I was glad to get down as I had used over three-quarters of my petrol.

*

The dangers in the autumn sky were still very real. On the afternoon of 1 November, B Flight, now commanded by an Australian, Flight Lieutenant Bob Bungay, was detached from A Flight as they climbed to 20,000 feet after the elusive 109s, then Nigel's voice came over the R/T:

'Red One, bandits overhead at 2 o'clock!'

As the Hurricanes banked towards them an unseen 109 dived on them and made a quick attack. As it broke away, Offenberg went after it, fired, and had the satisfaction of seeing the Messerschmitt go down streaming glycol. The German pilot eventually crash-landed near Selsey Bill to be taken prisoner. A week later Nigel Weir flew his last mission.

November 7 1940. At 1.50 pm, eleven aircraft of 145 were ordered to patrol near the Isle of Wight. Later they were told to return to base and patrol it at 20,000 feet. However, the enemy appeared – no less than an estimated fifty Me109s shadowing the Hurricanes in three formations, one ahead, one astern and the third to the south. 145 were unable to attack any of the three gaggles without exposing themselves to the others. The Hurricanes climbed but the 109s began to attack in pairs, picking off the rear pilots of B Flight. Five Hurricanes were shot down in this way. Flight Lieutenant Bungay went into the sea off St Laurence, IoW, and was injured. Sergeant D.B. Sykes crashed at Ventnor with injuries, while Sergeant J. McConnell went down over Wittering also being injured.

For some reason Nigel Weir was not flying his usual P2683; this being flown by Pilot Officer J.H. Ashton, while Weir flew P2720. Ashton went down to crash in the centre of the island near Ashley and it was initially thought that this was Weir because Weir's uncle, Philip Bartlett had given him a bullet-proof cushion marked with his name and this of course was in P2683. Weir, however had been hit and was seen to dive straight into the sea south-east of Woody Point off Ventnor and sank immediately. The rest of 145 got away, the remaining seven landed at 2.50. Nigel had been due to go on leave the next day, the leave referred to in his letter of 23 October.

The 109s which attacked 145 that day were JG2 aircraft. At 3.25 to 3.30 pm (German time) JG2 claimed six Hurricanes shot down from heights of between 21,400 to 24,600 feet. Major Helmut Wick, *Kommandeur* of JG2 claimed one, others being claimed by Oberleutnant Erich Leie (two), Oberleutnant Rudolf Pflanz, Leutnant Siegfried Schnell and Leutnant Heimberg.

Nigel's death was of course a terrible shock to his family but fate was to play two further severe blows before the war ended. Nigel's Wing Commander father died on 30 April 1941 when the ship in which he was travelling as OC troops was torpedoed John Weir, Nigel's younger brother, who was awarded the MC while serving with the 2nd Battalion of the Scots Guards, was killed in action at Anzio on 28 February 1944.

> There is a life in peace and strife
> Which everyone must live;
> We give our best and go to rest
> When we've no more to give.

3

Sandy

When the Battle of Britain began 'Sandy' Lane was a flight commander of a Spitfire squadron and by the end of the battle had taken command of it. Lane left us two records of his part in the fighting of 1940, firstly his flying log-book which can be seen and read in the Public Record Office at Kew in Surrey, and secondly a book. In 1942 his book *Spitfire – the Experiences of a Fighter Pilot* was published (John Murray, London). It is a little-known work and very much a product of the period, but nevertheless it is an extremely readable account of Lane's and his squadron's part in the battle. The name which appears as the author's is a pseudonym – Squadron Leader B.J. Ellen, a slight twisting of his real name.

In 1935, when he was eighteen years old, Brian John Edward Lane, son of Herbert and Bessie Lane, was working as a supervisor in an electric bulb company but the firm had to lay-off several workers and Lane was one of those they had to 'let go'. Out of a job he applied to join the Royal Air Force, was successful at his selection board interview, so on 22 March 1936 he arrived at an Elementary Flying School at Hamble. At the beginning of June he progressed to No 11 FTS at RAF Wittering where he stayed until January 1937, received his 'wings'; then on 8 January he was posted to 66 Squadron at Duxford flying Gloster Gauntlets. In March he volunteered to go to 213 Squadron, which was forming at Northolt and was soon to be commanded by Squadron Leader J.H. Edwards-Jones. He remained with 213 until September 1939 by which time the Gauntlets had been replaced by Hawker Hurricanes. Following his promotion to flight commander rank upon the outbreak of war, he was posted to 19 Squadron, which was equipped with Spitfires, and which had in fact been the first squadron to equip with Spitfires.

No 19 Squadron, commanded by Squadron Leader H.J. Cozens

AFC, was stationed at RAF Duxford. The commencement of hostilities with Germany was for the squadron, as it was for most squadrons, something of an anti-climax. Very little happened. There were no whirling dog-fights, no combats in the autumn sky, no hordes of enemy raiders bombing England. For Lane, leader of A Flight, it was very much a winter of discontent. However, all that quickly changed in May 1940 when the Germans finally took the offensive and invaded Holland, Belgium and France. There was some suggestion that the squadron might go to France but Dowding was firmly against any of his valuable Spitfires being thrown away across the Channel where clearly the fight was being lost. Instead, 19 Squadron moved to Hornchurch to help cover the subsequent evacuation of the British Expeditionary Force at the end of May. The BEF, overwhelmed and pushed back to the Channel coast near Dunkirk, had to be saved at all cost.

The squadron arrived at Hornchurch on 25 May. Everyone was keyed up for the morrow when patrols would be made over Dunkirk. Lane recorded that on the eve of his war, finally about to begin, he 'slept like a log'.

*

Squadron Leader G.D. Stephenson, who had taken over command of 19 Squadron back in January, led the squadron on its first war patrol over the Dunkirk operation the next morning. Lane, flying Spitfire N3040, recorded in his log-book:

> Squadron took-off 0740, arrived Calais 0750. Sighted 21 Ju87s over Calais. Red, Blue and Yellow sections attacked, Green section watching for escort. Got in a couple of attacks before Ball yelled 'Fighters!' and 30 Me109s descended on us. General dog-fight ensued. Saw Watson hit by cannon from Me109 and later parachute in water off Calais. Potter saw him bale out. I had a smack at various 109s and then got chased by three of them. Got a good burst at one doing a beam attack and he disappeared. Got away and headed for Hornchurch and a drink. Probable bag, one Ju87 and Me109. CO and Watson missing.

Nineteen Squadron claimed seven Ju87s and three 109s destroyed, plus a 109 probably destroyed for the loss of Stephenson and

Brian 'Sandy' Lane

Watson, with Eric Ball slightly wounded. Lane, modestly, claimed only probable victories but was later credited with two definite kills.

As acting CO, Lane led nine Spitfires out again at 2.45 pm (N3040). For some time the sky remained empty, then at around 4 o'clock whilst flying at 8,000 feet, the rear section reported eight Me109s a thousand feet higher. The Messerschmitts dived in a ragged formation and the squadron broke up to avoid them. Seeing one 109 dive after Flying Officer G.L. Sinclair, Lane went after it. The 109 missed its prey, levelled out above some cloud and headed for France. Lane followed, attacked from astern, letting go a 4-5 second burst from 300, down to 200 yards' range. The German fighter lurched onto its side and fell into a vertical dive. Lane went after it, pulling out finally at 2,500 feet, the 109 still falling well below him.

> Green 3 reported eight Me109s just above us off Calais. After Me109 chasing Sinclair into cloud, … pulled up and gave me a sitting target from below. Gave him a good burst which he ran into. He went straight down. I followed him but pulled out at 3,000 feet and he must have gone straight in. Blacked out completely pulling out in time. Landed at Manston and stayed for tea. Lovely by the coast in this weather. Took-off from Manston with Sergeant Jennings – landed Hornchurch and found Lynn missing. Later heard he had landed on Walmers beach with a bullet through his knee – OK.

Sergeant Irwin also failed to get back, but Lane, George Petre and Gordon Sinclair had all claimed Me109s. At 5.45 am the following morning, the 27th, the squadron again patrolled Calais/Dunkirk but it was all quiet. At 11 am they repeated the performance:

> Flight Sergeant Unwin and Sergeants Potter and Jennings. Sighted He111 and attacked over Gravelines. Heavy AA fire. Chased Heinkel in and out of cloud mass and put all ammo into him – no visible effect. Return fire from top gun stopped after first burst and I think there must have been one Hun less in the world. Unwin was separated from me and I was set upon by three Me110s.

That evening, again with Flight Sergeant 'Grumpy' Unwin, who was to be one of the squadron's must successful pilots in 1940, and Flying Officer Frankie Brinsden, Lane was over Dunkirk, slightly inland from the coast.

> Found one Henschel 126 and chased him. Twisted and turned like hell and after a couple of bursts I lost him. Brinsden had a crack at him and Unwin got him and pushed him into the deck after Brinsden and I had reformed. Returned from Ypres to Dunkirk right down on the deck and have never seen anything so peaceful. No sign of war at all except the usual smoke pall over Dunkirk.

*

Until now 19 Squadron, like most other units, operated at just squadron strength although quite often more than one squadron joined forces during battles over Dunkirk. On 28 May, in an attempt to try and not be constantly out-numbered by the enemy opposition, all three fighter squadrons at Hornchurch flew out in wing formation.

> Balbo patrol over Dunkirk with 54, 65 and 19. Nothing seen but one Lysander – poor sod! No escort or anything.

Later in the day:

> Same Balbo ran into fifty Me109s. Got into these with top flight and got a nice shot at one enemy aircraft. Fired about twenty rounds when guns stopped. Another EA was just getting on my tail so didn't wait but half rolled and left the party. Discovered I had no air pressure so came home. Flight Sergeant Unwin and Sergeant Potter bagged three Dornier 215s, Unwin bagged a 109.

At dawn on 29 May:

> 19, 54 and 65 Balbo – all quiet. Huns don't seem to get up very early.

Nos 54 and 65 Squadrons moved out of Hornchurch, being

replaced by 222 and 41 Squadrons. 19, as senior squadron, began to lead the wing formation but it was not until 1 June that they made contact.

Flying K9799, Lane, with his squadron, plus 222 and 41 and 616 (the latter being based at Rochford, Hornchurch's satellite airfield) were off at 4.20 am. One hour and twenty minutes later, two miles north-east of Dunkirk at 4,400 feet, Lane spotted 12 Me110s and led the squadron in line astern as the 110s turned towards the coast. Lane chased and attacked one Messerschmitt, saw one of its engines jerk to a stop, while the other motor poured glycol. The 110 dived earthwards and had not pulled out when last seen at about fifty feet. Lane turned after another 110, attacking it from head-on, his fire appearing to enter the Messerschmitt's nose. Then it passed below his Spitfire and he lost sight of it.

Ran into twelve Me110s straight from FTS I should think. Terrific sport. I got one definitely as he went down with one engine stopped and the other streaming coolant. He did not appear to pull out at fifty feet but did not actually see him crash.

Back at base the claims amounted to seven 110s shot down plus three Me109s with whom B Flight, under Wilf Clouston, had had a private scrap higher up. Tubby Mermagen, CO of 222 Squadron, had shot the tail off a 110 from an incredible 1,200 yards' range! He told the others that once his sights were on he had 'stirred' his stick around the cockpit, thereby achieving a hosepipe effect with his eight .303 machine-guns, which had sliced right through the Messerschmitt's tail. Later that morning the wing flew out again, Lane recording the following experience in his log-book:

Most amazing sight this evacuation. Thames barges, sailing boats, anything that will float, and the Navy. God help them down there, they need more than we can give them. Ran into a bunch of Do215s and He111s, thin layer of 10/10ths cloud at 4,000 feet, made things a bit difficult, as the sods kept diving into cloud. Tore round firing at Heinkels as they appeared behind cloud but couldn't do much as windscreen was completely oiled up. Headed for home at sea level along the line of ships. Passed a Channel steamer and saw the sea erupt just behind him. Nearly jumped out of the cockpit. I looked up and saw a Do215 cruising along at 2,000 feet right on top of me it seemed. I had no ammo and low on petrol so I could do nothing about it. S/L Hood, 41, (Squadron Leader H.R.L. Hood) reported the same thing but he met his Hun at sea level. He made a stab as if to attack and the wretched Boche fell into the sea without a shot being fired. Was his face red.

Again the squadron had some success, two destroyed and three probables for one pilot missing but he was later fished out of the sea. Lane could not claim the first Dornier he had attacked although he thought he'd damaged it. His Spitfire, K9799, had been hit in the wing and of course the airscrew had leaked oil onto the windscreen.

The next day another wing Balbo to Dunkirk, but all appeared quiet. The evacuation was ending. On 5 June the squadron returned to Duxford where the new CO, Squadron Leader P.C. Pinkham, took over from Lane. Under Lane's temporary leadership, 19 Squadron had claimed 28 enemy planes destroyed plus nine probables, for the loss of just three pilots plus another wounded. He took a well-deserved 48 hours leave with his wife Eileen.

*

June and July were taken up with patrols and flights at night chasing nocturnal raiders, a tiring and unrewarding pastime. One bright spot was that Brian Lane received notification of the award of the DFC on 31 July, not only for leading the squadron over Dunkirk but for his personal prowess. In his log-book his assessment as a fighter pilot was judged as 'exceptional' by his immediate superiors, and his air gunnery as 'above the average'.

Then the Battle of Britain began, but it was 11 Group in the south that took the brunt of the early attacks. 19 Squadron, having moved to Fowlmere, in Cambridgeshire, missed these early rounds and indeed began to feel they would miss all the action, especially when in early August they flew further north to RAF Coltishall to fly protective convoy patrols. On 16 August Lane's A Flight was, however, scrambled in the late afternoon, Lane flying a cannon armed Spitfire, R6919. (19 Squadron was asked to test and report on the use of 20mm cannons and they caused several problems in these early stages of development.)

> Investigated X-raid above cloud with several aircraft of A Flight. Turned out to be about 150 Huns. Waded into escort of Me110s but ruddy cannons stopped on me. Unwin and Potter got one each.

After weeks of inactivity, it was a real tonic to get back into action. They had seen wave after wave of He111s but they had turned tail when the Spitfires appeared, leaving Lane and his men to fight off the Messerschmitts. Lane believed he hit one 110 before his guns failed but in his usually modest way made no real claim. Just over a week later, on 24 August, the squadron saw further action.

Again in R6919, Lane, with the squadron, took-off at 3.45 pm, Lane leading with Red Section. At about 4 o'clock when over North Weald, AA fire was observed to the east and Lane turned towards it, at the same time seeing a number of enemy aircraft above at 15,000 feet. Ten minutes later, having climbed steadily, he got astern of a somewhat ragged formation of about forty Me110s and Dorniers, with ten Me109s above and behind. Although he had been unable to gain a more favourable height, Lane nevertheless led the Spitfires in, attacking from below and from the starboard side, being almost within range before the 110 saw them and turned in their direction. A dog-fight began: Lane fired from below and behind the nearest 110 but then tracer shells arced over his head and he rapidly broke away. Getting below another Messerschmitt he fired into its port engine and saw a large part of the engine or mainplane fly off. The 110 dived, and Lane watched as it crashed into the sea. As he recorded humorously in his book when escaping from the first 110, he felt like a replica of the famous advertisement – 'That's Shell, that was!'

> Ran into a bunch of Huns over Estuary. Had a peck at an Me110 but had to break away as tracer was coming over my head from another behind me. He appeared to be hitting his fellow countryman in front of me but I didn't wait to see if he shot him

down. I looked round at another and shot his engine right out of the wing – lovely. Crashed near North Foreland. Last trip in 'Blitzen III'.

'Blitzen III' was obviously the name he had given R6919. After this fight he came across a crippled Me110 with one engine stopped. He slid in behind it but as he pressed the gun button found his guns were empty. The fortunate 110 pilot, with apparently no rear-man in evidence, flew on oblivious of how lucky he had been.

*

At the beginning of September Lane went off on leave, returning on the 5th. 19 Squadron had been scrambled that Thursday morning and had lost its CO, Squadron Leader Pinkham, shot down by Me109s near Hornchurch. Two other Spitfires had been damaged. Flight Lieutenant B.J.E. Lane DFC again took over the squadron but this time it was official and he was promoted to squadron leader rank.

He first led the squadron as its new boss on 7 September, the day the Luftwaffe dropped bombs on London for the first time. On the second patrol of the day, at about 5 pm, AA fire was observed over North Weald, and then a formation of 20 bombers and 50 fighters flying east at 15,000 feet came into view. 19 Squadron was now part of the 12 Group Wing as instigated by the CO of 242 Squadron, Douglas Bader, and the AOC of 12 Group, Air Vice Marshal Trafford Leigh-Mallory. When the enemy were seen, Bader led the attack followed by 310 Czech Squadron and then 19 Squadron. Messerschmitts began to dive down, one Me110 diving straight in front of Lane's Spitfire (P9386 QV-K). He led his flight after it but two Hurricanes also went for it. Lane opened fire as did the other aircraft and then the two-man crew simply baled out, one parachute failing to open. The 110 crashed one mile east of Hornchurch, the surviving German being taken prisoner. This 110 was from I/ZG2. 19 Squadron claimed a total of four Germans down for no loss, the Wing claiming about twenty in total.

Lane was in action again on the 11th. Ten minutes after take-off at 3.40 pm (again in P9386), the Wing, consisting of 19, 611 and 74 Squadrons, having climbed to 23,000 feet over North Weald, saw the inevitable AA fire. Just south of Gravesend they saw a large formation of enemy aircraft flying northwards, three thousand feet below. Sandy Lane turned south and dived in a head-on attack at the leading formation consisting of 12 Heinkel 111s. Turning to port he saw the bombers turning south-east over Sittingbourne. There were now only seven Heinkels with two more half a mile or so ahead, and two white nosed Me110s astern and to port. Lane attacked the rear Messerschmitt, his fire blasting large pieces off its starboard engine which promptly stopped. The 110 broke to one side and following Lane's next attack the starboard engine burst into flames and the 110 dived. Lane was after the other 110 but it rapidly dived away leaving the Heinkels behind. Lane again attacked the Heinkels head-on, then from the beam. One of them at the rear was hit, and its starboard engine began to burn, but Lane then ran out of ammunition.

> Party over London, 19 leading 611 and 74. Sighted big bunch of Huns south of River and got a lovely head-on attack on two leading He111s. Broke them up and picked up a small bunch of six with 110s as escort. Found myself alone with these lads so proceeded to have a bit of sport. Got one of the 110s on fire whereupon the other left his charges and ran for home. Attacking He111s, finally caught one in both engines. Never had so much fun before.

Then came the big day – 15 September. During the morning the Wing fought Dornier and Messerschmitts, although Lane, attacking several made no claims. Then he spotted some Dorniers lower down already under attack from Wing aircraft. Several fighters could be seen attacking one Dornier and he joined in, then watched as it gradually went down, its crew baling out. It narrowly missed a house and finally plunged into the ground.

In the afternoon, 19 Squadron was off at 2.10 pm, with Lane leading in X4170. Yet again AA fire showed the way, then thirty Dorniers swam into view. Lane led the squadron up to attack the fighter escort at 30,000 feet. A loose dog-fight ensued with three Me109s, then more dived down from the blue. He saw two 109s above and one swooped to attack him. Lane got onto its tail and during a terrific scrap, fired several short bursts. The 109 took violent evasive action and its pilot made for clouds. Lane, following, got in another burst – five seconds, and the 109 flicked over and inverted, entered cloud in a shallow dive, out of control. He then flew south and attacked two formations of thirty Dornier 17s from behind, then from head-on, until his ammunition was finished.

> Party, 242 leading Wing. Ran into the whole of the Luftwaffe over 10/10ths over London. Wave after wave of bombers covered by several hundred fighters. Waded into escort as per arrangement and picked out a 109. Had a hell of a dog-fight and finally he went into cloud in an inverted dive. Pretty obvious he crashed as he appeared out of control. Sky seemed empty so went down to Dungeness to wait for the lads coming home. Saw large formation of 215s and had a smack at each without result.

The squadron lost the veteran Sergeant J.A. Potter during this battle, being shot down by 109s, and two other Spitfires were damaged. However, Potter was later reported a prisoner so must have chased the Germans out to sea before being hit.

Three days later, on the 18th, Lane was late in getting from his office to dispersal and missed the scramble and another big fight. Flight Lieutenant W.J. Lawson, who took Lane's Spitfire (X4170), was hit in the glycol tank and had to force land at Eastchurch but was unhurt. 19 Squadron and the Wing still had fights in September but Lane had no further successes as the battle came to an end. On 8 November during another Wing patrol they saw some Me109s over Canterbury and gave chase. Unfortunately a Hurricane squadron chased them and the leader put a burst into Lane's engine (P7377), the culprit was

> apparently CO of one of the North Weald squadrons, blacked out and minus oxygen. Jennings escorted me down and refused to leave me. Damn good of him.

Just a week later, 15 November, flying P7434, during a mid-morning convoy patrol off Felixstowe with 242 Squadron, Lane spotted exhaust plumes to the south at 35,000 feet, some fifteen miles apart. Sending Blue Section after one with Yellow Section above to cut it off, Lane and Red Section proceeded after the other one, climbing south to get between the enemy aircraft and the sun.

19 Squadron, early 1940. Lane is on the extreme left. Others identified are: F/Sgt Unwin 5th from left, Sgt H. Steere, 6th, FO Frankie Brinsden 7th, Squdn Ldr H.J. Cozens 9th and F/Lt Wilf Clousten 11th.

19 Squadron during the Battle: l to r: Sgt D. Fulford, Sandy Lane on wing with "Flash", Grumpy Unwin, F/LT?, S/Ldr Billy Burton (616 Sqdn), FO Brinsden on wing, unknown.

After a twenty minute chase up the Estuary, the German saw the approaching Spitfires, turned and dived. Lane turned with it and ordered the section into line astern. Lane closed with the German at 8,000 feet and opened fire. Pieces of what appeared to be cowling flew off the machine and coolant appeared from the port motor. As he broke away he saw Red 3 attack and then flames came from the German's starboard engine. The enemy machine, a Messerschmitt 110, continued down, Lane attacking again, then it dived into the sea off Southend.

> Wing patrol. Sighted two exhaust plumes over Dunkirk heading north-west. Broke away, B Flight taking rear one. Broke Unwin with Yellow Section away to lead B Flight. They got it. Continued with Red Section and Pilot Officer Cunningham after another Hun which was a 110. After a Cook's tour up the Estuary, caught him at 35,000 feet. He dived – idiot, and closed to 8,000 feet, got his port engine. Jock (Pilot Officer W. Cunningham DFC) came in and set his starboard one alight and he went in in the middle of a convoy in the Estuary.

*

That was the end of the battle for Sandy Lane. The following winter months were taken up with night sorties, trying to find the elusive enemy raiders in the blackness over London and the south. By the end of 1940, Lane, the veteran squadron commander, had over 885 flying hours in his log-book. Yet his experience had been hard won. He was physically tired, and the tiredness shows in photographs taken of him at the time. By the spring of 1941, when Fighter Command was beginning to look towards France in order to continue their fight with the Luftwaffe, Lane was nearing the end of his time with 19 Squadron. He was involved in some of the early sweeps, his last being flown on 30 June. He flew P7619 and his squadron was part of Wing Commander Bob Tuck's Duxford Wing. With 19, 56 and 257 Squadrons, Lane patrolled from Boulogne to Hardelot at 25,000 feet but they found the sky empty of Germans. They saw their Stirling bombers coming out of France through a veritable wall of flak, then the Spitfires turned for West Malling and home. It was during this period that he finished writing his book.

Leaving 19 Squadron, Sandy Lane went to 12 Group Headquarters at Hucknall until November when he was sent overseas. At first he was with Air HQ, Western Desert until February 1942 when he took a post at HQ Middle East until June. By the summer of 1942 he was keen to get back to operational flying, having 'flown' a desk for quite long enough. His wish granted, he returned to England going to 61 OTU at Montford Bridge, then in December he was given command of 167 Squadron at RAF Ludham in Norfolk. He arrived at his new command on 9 December. Four days later he flew his first operational sortie since June 1941.

At 3.10 pm Squadron Leader Brian Lane DFC took-off with three other pilots to fly a Rhubarb over Holland. Their target was the railway between Noerdyk – Bergen Op Zoom. The Dutch coast was crossed between Voorne and Goederee at 3.50, his companions being Flying Officer J.L. Plesman (VL-P), Pilot Officer W.G. Evans (VL-V), and Flying Officer H.P.J. Henkensfeldt-Jansen (VL-R). Lane was flying Spitfire VL-U.

Over the Dutch coast they followed the Hollandseh Diep, meeting some intense flak from Hellevoetsluis, Willemstad, Moerdyk Bridge and from the north shore of the Hollandseh Diep. When two or three miles south-west of Zierizee, two Focke Wulf 190s came in behind the four Spitfires. Flying Officer Plesman went forward to the starboard side of Lane to draw his attention to the two enemy fighters. The 190s opened fire at Plesman and Lane from 3-400 yards. Plesman next saw his CO behind a Focke Wulf which was turning inland to the south-east. They were just south-west of Zierizee and as he appeared to be all right, Plesman turned to help Pilot Officer Evans who was under attack. The danger passed, Plesman and Evans looked for Lane but to no avail.

Sandy Lane died that December day and the exact location of his last resting place is not known; he just disappeared. Whether he lies in the grave of an unknown airman, or whether he crashed into one of the many sea inlets is not known for certain. He was twenty-five years old. What is certain is that the RAF lost one of its most dedicated squadron commanders and fighter pilots.

4

David

There was another fighter pilot whose log-books survive and who also left us with a book of his experiences of 1940. David Moore Crook, son of William and Winifred Moore Crook, wrote *Spitfire Pilot* in 1942 (Faber & Faber Ltd). Rather better known than Sandy Lane's book, it had several impressions published and was even reprinted only a few years ago. It is a splendid story, well written, highly descriptive and amazingly free from censorship, even though, like Lane's book there was the wartime need to conceal the real names of his squadron comrades. Fortunately, most if not all are identifiable with a little research.

David Crook was a weekend airman, an Auxiliary. Living in Huddersfield, after completing his education at Cambridge, he became a member of 609 'West Riding' squadron of the Auxiliary Air Force at Yeadon in August 1938. He was in the midst of learning to fly when war came the following year and he was called-up. He was sent off to No 6 Flying Training School at Little Rissington, Gloucestershire, completing his training, and was then returned to 609 in May 1940, the squadron being based at Drem in Scotland. By this time he was a man with responsibilities; he had married Dorothy on 23 August 1939, and had a whole day for a honeymoon before mobilization was ordered.

Back with the squadron, and now fully operational, everyone became highly excited and eager to move south when news came through that the Germans had invaded the low countries. Crook was so excited that a day or so later, jumping eagerly out of bed, he pulled a ligament in his left knee. This put him in hospital while his squadron got the order to move to Northolt just north-west of London from where it flew operations over Dunkirk. However, he improved after an operation and by the end of June rejoined 609 at Northolt.

When the opening rounds of the Battle of Britain commenced,

609 had moved to Middle Wallop using Warmwell as an advanced base. It was from Warmwell, on 9 July, that David Crook first met the enemy. He had already flown one abortive sortie, then at around 6.30 pm, he was sent off again to the Weymouth area when hostile aircraft were reported attacking shipping in the Channel. Crook was flying in the number three slot of the section, flying Spitfire P9322 (PR-L). Like Sandy Lane, Crook used his logbook as something of a diary.

> After about 45 minutes patrol over Portland we sighted two Ju87s climbing into the clouds on our left. We turned towards them, I was flying No 3, when I saw above me at least nine Me110s diving on us. I warned the others and then when the leading 110 opened fire I turned off very sharply to the left and dived through cloud. A Ju87 flew across my sights at close range and I gave him a burst. He seemed to go right through it. I then climbed up again and fired without result at an Me110 who immediately dived into cloud and I lost him. I found myself very near to a Ju87 so stalked it through cloud and when it emerged into clear sky I fired all the rest of my ammunition at very close range. He turned over and dived in flames into the sea.

The Messerschmitts which Crook had seen, attacked his two companions, Pilot Officers Michael Appelby and Peter Drummond Hay. Both pilots had left their radios on 'transmit' and thus did not hear Crook's urgent yell that 110s were behind them. Appelby luckily, just switched over to hear just the word 'Messerschmitts' and quickly turned away. Drummond-Hay, however, flew on and failed to return.

Crook's Stuka which he shot down was piloted by a *Staffel Kapitän* of I/StG77, Hauptmann Friedrich-Karl Freiherr von Dalwigk zu Lichtenfels, aged thirty-three. Von Dalwigk, known to his friends as 'Chicken', had joined the Luftwaffe in 1933 and by 1939 he had considerable experience as a dive-bomber pilot. He flew in Poland and France as well as the opening stages of the Battle against England. He was awarded a posthumous Knight's Cross on 21 July.

The loss of his friend Drummond-Hay affected David Crook deeply; he had even been his room-mate. In his book he paints a poignant scene when returning to their room to see Peter's towel still on the window ledge where he had tossed it casually earlier that morning. Now he was dead, in the cockpit of his Spitfire at the bottom of the Channel. He was unable to sleep in the room, and so he moved his things into Gordon Mitchell's room. Then Peter's wife telephoned to check on a trip Peter and she had planned. Flight Lieutenant 'Pip' Barron, their flight commander, had had to tell her the sad news.

Crook then went off on a 24-hour leave with his wife. When he returned he found that both Barron and Mitchell had been killed over the Channel. Mitchell had been at Cambridge with Crook, was a hockey blue, a fine athlete and an only son.

Two days later, Saturday 13 July, David Crook was involved in another skirmish, this time over southern England flying Spitfire N3023.

> Intercepted Dornier 215 over Devizes. Gunner opened fire but I gave him a long burst which must have k.o'd him as there was no subsequent reply to our fire. He finally escaped into cloud.

On 27 July, Pilot Officer J.R. Buchanan was shot down and killed by Me109s over Weymouth Bay whilst flying N3023. The Channel battles came to an end, the main assault of the battle was about to begin.

*

During the first week of August, 609 had to be content merely to chase elusive, high flying German aeroplanes over the south east corner of England. On the 8th, however, in brilliant sunshine, they were patrolling above a convoy off the Isle of Wight. On their second patrol, Crook became separated in some small layers of cloud and then found himself in the midst of battle. He dived towards a Messerschmitt 109 but a Hurricane shot it down before he could close. This was his only real chance in the fight in which earlier subject Nigel Weir was more successful. David Crook, however, was to fare better on the 11th.

Flying R6986 (PR-S) as number three in Green Section, Crook and 609 were off at 9.45 am, heading for Swanage. Shortly before 10.15, when fifteen miles south-east of Swanage they found the enemy. Immediately his section leader turned to the left, climbing hard into the sun. Control instructed them to climb to 18,000 feet which would be sufficient to get above the raiders but at 25,000 feet some fighters were still high above them. As No 3, Crook was keeping a keen look-out behind, but in doing so failed to see Green 1 and 2 make a turn and he found himself alone. Quite a few twin-engined Me110s were milling about below him but one, some short distance from the others, attracted his attention. Crook dived down on it, opened fire from the beam but was unable to get sufficient deflection owing to the steepness of the 110's desperate turn. Staying with the Messerschmitt, Crook stuck to its tail, being so close that he had to throttle back to avoid a collision. He fired again from practically point-blank-range whereupon the 110 turned to the right, appeared to stall, then began to roll over onto its back. With a slowing 110 right in front of him, Crook had to take violent evasive action to avoid hitting the German aeroplane, especially its starboard wing, as the 110 turned over, then went down.

> We took-off at 0945 and after patrolling round Warmwell saw some smoke trails out to sea. Investigated and found a large force of Me110s circling round in circles at 25,000 feet, Hurricanes already engaging them. We all attacked separately. I climbed well above the scrum and then saw an Me110 some distance from the others. I dived on him and fired a burst from the quarter which missed as I could not get sufficient deflection. I then came into very close range and fired. This hit him and he did a climbing turn to the right, stalled and started to turn over. I narrowly missed colliding with him and did not see him again. Found myself with Me's all around so dived away as hard as I could and returned to Warmwell.

However, it appears that this 110, like five others from ZG/2, were all destroyed, five by 609, one by 145 Squadron, all over Portland at between 10.10 and 10.35 am. Initially, Crook was credited with only a probable.

The following day, the 'Glorious Twelfth' – the day before the Germans were to launch their great air offensive, Crook and 609 were again in action. Portland was once again to be the scene of the air battle with Luftwaffe fighters flying 'free chases' (*frei Jagd*) over

P/o D.M.CROOK. D.F.C.   609 SQUADRUN

David Crook

Kent soon after dawn. Later, radar stations were attacked, in an attempt to blind the RAF fighter controllers, then two small convoys in the Channel. Soon after mid-day a huge armada of German Ju88s and Me110s swept towards the Isle of Wight area.

David Crook was about to start a 24-hour leave period when 609 were called to instant readiness. It was 11 o'clock and Crook was shaving. Wiping the soap from his face he joined the others and shortly afterwards they were scrambled. Switching on his R/T whilst taxiing out he found the radio dead, so was forced to remain on the ground for several minutes before a loose wire was located and connected, then he was off.

He climbed towards the Isle of Wight, seeing AA bursts to the left of Portsmouth. He flew to investigate but could see nothing, then suddenly spotted three layers of fighters milling around between 22,000 and 26,000 feet over the eastern end of the island. He continued to climb up above the middle layer of circling Me110s, selected a target and put the stick forward. Diving to within range he thumbed the gun-button in a quick deflection shot, seeing his bullets either hitting or passing very close around the Messerschmitt. Closing right in – he always got in close – he narrowly avoided a collision, but lost sight of the 110 as he broke away and continued down for 3,000 feet. Pulling out, a 110, enveloped in a sheet of flame, dived vertically past him within 200 yards. Crook felt certain this was his 110 as he could see no other RAF aircraft near him. He had damaged both his wings due to his high speed dive so decided to continue down and return home, where, upon landing, he hit a bump which tore the landing light out of the wing. The Spitfire, N3024 (PR-H), had to be returned to the factory for repairs.

Big attack on Portsmouth. We took-off from Wallop and I followed about five minutes later owing to R/T trouble. I did not see any of the squadron again during the action. Climbed towards the Isle of Wight, saw AA fire over Portland and a fire raging in the dockyard. Could not see any bombers there. Saw large enemy force off the east end of the IoW, Me109s and 110s in three layers circling around at 23,000 feet. I climbed above middle layer, selected a machine and dived onto him and opened fire and saw my bullets either hit him or narrowly miss. Almost collided, and lost sight of him as I continued my dive. I pulled out about 3,000 feet below and at that moment a 110 in a sheet of flames dived past me within 200 yards. This machine was certainly destroyed but don't know if it was mine. I think it quite probably was as did not see any other British fighters in action when I attacked. When I pulled out of my dive found myself in a very vulnerable position with many enemy around and above, and so dived away hard, saw over 500 mph IAS (Indicated Air Speed), actual speed probably nearly 600 mph. Almost blacked out as I pulled out and later found the wings damaged and landing lamp torn out of wing. My Spitfire went back to the factory for new pair of wings.

Number 609 Squadron claimed seven Germans shot down for no loss. The following day – the 13th, the Luftwaffe launched its '*Adler Tag*' – Eagle Day. The mad, hectic pace of the air battles continued. David Crook flew R6699 (PR-L). It was a good day for the squadron.

Best effort yet for 609. Took-off 3.30 pm and climbed through cloud. After patrolling for some time during which I could hear a lot of German talk on the R/T. We sighted a large number, 60 or 70, Me109s and Ju87s approaching. We climbed above them with Blue Section (Flight Lieutenant J.H.G. McArthur, Flying Officer T. Nowierski [Polish] and Crook) as top guard. Suddenly I saw a few Me109s pass beneath us. I immediately broke away and attacked one which was some distance behind the rest. I came up behind and fired a good burst from dead astern. He rocked violently and then turned over and dived away and burst into flames and crashed near Hardy's Monument behind Weymouth. Just before we attacked I heard a German voice (presumably a Wing Commander) saying repeatedly, '*Achtung, achtung, Spit und Hurri.*' He sounded a bit put out about something.

Crook's victim on this occasion has been identified as a pilot from II Gruppe of JG53, Heinz Pfannschmidt, who died in the crash. Crook followed the Messerschmitt down, saw it burning in a field and people from a nearby village coming out of their houses to see it. Again 609 had no casualties but they did claim a total of 13 victories.

David Crook was in action again the next day, the fourth day in succession. Not that this was anything unusual, for all operational pilots in the southern Groups of Fighter Command were constantly in the air during the summer of 1940, often flying three, four, even six sorties each day. This time, however, the Luftwaffe came right onto 609's doorstep – Middle Wallop. Three German bombers, Heinkel 111s of KG55 bombed 609's hangars and offices, three airmen, who ran to close the doors of one hangar, being killed when the doors were blown down on top of them.

Sergeant A.N. Feary was in the air and attacked a Ju88 not far from base, and then Crook and John Dundas got into the air amid the smoke and caught up with the Heinkels. Crook fired at two of them, firing a ten-second burst at one whilst closing to thirty yards. Dundas followed up the attack although Crook became separated in cloud. The Heinkel subsequently crashed and was found to have been flown by Oberst Alois Stoeckl, *Geschwader Kommandeur* of KG55. Two other bodies recovered from the wreck belonged to Oberst G. Frank, Chief of Staff of Luftgau VIII attached to V Fliegerkorps, and Oberleutnant Brossler, KG55's navigation specialist.

> Wallop bombed by single Ju88 which hit a hangar – shot down about two miles away. We took off as bombs fell and patrolled aerodrome for some time and fired without apparent results at two He111s which I saw north in clouds. Unfortunately Goodwin [Flying Officer Harry Goodwin] was missing and we never knew really what happened to him. His body was washed up on the Isle of Wight ten days later. He must have chased a Hun out to sea and been shot down.

A victory the next day was one which David Crook was not credited with.

> Middle Wallop again bombed, this time by a fairly large force of Ju88s and Me110s. We shot down four 110s confirmed. A Blenheim attacked the German formation and I shot him down by mistake. Crew OK (save for cut on rear gunner's bottom) –

machine landed at Wallop looking very well peppered. Not a very good show!

The Blenheim crew from 604 Squadron, also based at Wallop, was putting in some practice flying and decided to have a go when the formation of Ju88s came onto the scene. Crook had got in amongst the Junkers and chose the similar looking twin-engined Bristol Blenheim and opened up on it.

On 23 August Crook and his wife Dorothy celebrated their first wedding anniversary. The war too was nearing the end of its first year.

Flying PR-P on the 25th, Crook with 609 raced towards Swanage during the afternoon. While Hurricanes from 17 and 87 Squadrons attacked Ju88s and Me110s, 609's Spitfires took on other 110s and the more dangerous and agile Me109 single seaters. Crook recorded in his log-book:

> Big fight over Warmwell. Dived much too fast on a Me110 and blazed away but missed and overshot badly. His gunner got three bullets through my wing-root within two feet of me. I learnt not to be over enthusiastic after this show and always took my time. Much better and safer.

Number 609 Squadron destroyed two 110s, damaged several others and also shot down a brace of 109s for the cost of two damaged Spitfires. 17 and 87 also scored heavily; one colourful pilot in 17 Squadron, Count Manfred Czernin, claimed three 110s which won for him the DFC. Flight Lieutenant Ian Gleed of 87 Squadron also scored two 110 victories, bringing his personal score to 11.

Crook was very fed up at missing his 110 which had been right in front of him – a sitter, but the lesson it taught him was to be more cool in future and to take his time.

It was, however, some time before he was to have another chance and an opportunity to be cooler. With leave, poor weather and the battles moving nearer to London, Crook had no chance to get to grips with the enemy until 27 September, again over Swanage.

Crook was flying as Blue 3 in Spitfire R6961. They were scrambled at 11.15 am, but Crook became separated before the enemy was engaged. When the Germans were found, Yellow

Section turned towards them to attack and Crook went with them. The enemy aeroplanes were flying round in an anti-clockwise circle. Crook came round into an attacking position behind a 110 but his turn proved too tight and he spun off. Levelling out and recovering, he regained height, finding the enemy's defensive circle broken and the hostile aircraft – Me110s – streaming out to sea. Choosing one of the retreating Messerschmitts, he soon overhauled it but the alert rear-gunner was firing in his direction. Crook jabbed the gun-button and the return fire ceased abruptly. With nothing now to deter him, Crook closed in and emptied his guns into the 110, aiming carefully at both engines in turn and then raking the fuselage. Smoke began to pour from the port engine, then another Spitfire came in and finished off the crippled fighter. Crook watched as, with one motor stopped it went down and crashed into the sea.

> In fight at 25,000 feet above Swanage. Miller killed in action – collided with a 110. I chased one out to sea, put out rear-gunner and started his port motor smoking furiously – out of ammo. Bidsee arrived and finished it off.

The 110 was shared between Crook and Flying Officer J.D. Bisdee, and as Crook mentioned, one pilot was lost. Pilot Officer R.F.G. Miller crashed after the collision with the 110 near Weymouth Bay. Crook had been flying just behind Mick Miller, saw him turn towards an on-coming 110, neither pilot giving way. With a closing speed estimated at 600 mph, Miller and the Messerschmitt hit and exploded. Miller's brother was lost on a bombing raid in July 1940.

Again in his book, Crook reflected in the loss of yet another friend, recalling when he sat down for lunch shortly after landing that it had only just been a few short hours earlier that he had sat, breakfasted and chatted with Miller, everything being quite normal. Now he too was no more.

Three days later, Monday the 30th, Crook had his greatest day. At 11 o'clock 609 took-off for Swanage; Crook was leading Green Section in X4165. Thirty minutes later, the squadron went into line astern, with Green Section closing in behind Blue Section. A moment or two later a few Me109s flew across the Spitfires' line of flight at about the same level. 609 turned after them and seeing the danger, the Messerschmitts began to dive. 609 pursued them eagerly, Crook selecting one, his speed rising to around 600 mph as he closed. Catching the 109 and zooming up from below and behind when the German began to flatten out, Crook gave him a good long burst. The Messerschmitt, mortally hit, turned over and with smoke streaming out, dived straight into the sea.

Looking round he saw another 109 to his right begin to disintegrate – Pilot Officer Mike Appelby's victim. Crook spotted another German fighter heading south towards France and gave chase. He quickly overhauled this second 109, got right behind it and opened fire. The 109's canopy flew off, flashing back and over Crook's own cockpit cover; then the German turned over and dived. Expecting the 109 to go right into the water, Crook was surprised to see it flatten out and begin to climb up again although it had begun to leave a trail of glycol smoke. Making no mistake, Crook caught it up, fired, and watched as the 109 crashed into the Channel about twenty-five miles from the French coast.

Crook recorded that he felt distinctly reluctant when finishing off this 109, feeling some kindred sympathy for the German pilot in his crippled fighter plane. Yet he knew that if mercy was shown, this same pilot might easily return on the morrow, shoot down RAF pilots, possibly a close friend. That was when his thumb had pressed down the gun button, situated on the control column, to start his eight .303 machine-guns firing.

In the mid-afternoon of the 30th, 609 was off once again. Crook and his section was ordered to investigate some aeroplanes seen below which proved to be Me109s. Coming down from the sun they surprised the Messerschmitt pilots – a near perfect bounce. Crook selected one and dog-fought it for some time over and out from Weymouth. Hit finally, the 109 began to spiral down trailing coolant, but then it was lost in cloud. Crook's own words recorded both actions, first the morning sortie:

We intercepted some Me109s at 23,000 feet over Swanage. The fools tried to escape by diving and we all went down after them. I got up to about 600 mph and easily caught mine, gave it a burst and he crashed into the sea. I then chased another one and put him into the sea about twenty-five miles from Cherbourg. It took

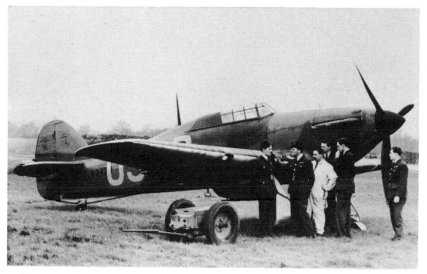

Hawker Hurricane of 56 Squadron. Victor Beamish flew several sorties with this squadron from North Weald.

Three frames from a camera-gun film showing the destruction of an Me110 during the Battle.

me a long time to get back to the English coast and pleased to see white cliffs.

Of the afternoon show:

> I was leading Green Section and we attacked six Me109s ten miles north of Poole. I had a very enjoyable few minutes dog-fighting with one and though behind him all the time could not get sights properly on him. Finally he dived for cloud, but I chased him to Weymouth and then gave him a good burst. He turned over onto his back and spun into cloud streaming glycol and smoke. I could not claim him as definite as I did not see him actually crash but he certainly never got back to France. This was my best day yet.

It also proved to be his last real action. Although he remained with 609 Squadron until November he made no further combat claims. Yet his work was rewarded on 17 October when he received the Distinguished Flying Cross. He flew with the squadron, trying to combat the high flying and often elusive 109s during the autumn of 1940, flying his last operation on 8 November in X4165. The very next day he sat for Cuthbert Orde, having his portrait drawn by this famous artist who had been commissioned by the Air Ministry to capture in charcoal the faces of Britain's famous airmen. In his log-book he recorded his last sortie:

> Last op. with squadron and as CO away I led the squadron. Got up to 32,000 feet but 109s still above us! Unfortunately nothing happened.

There had been another important event on the 8th; his son Nicholas was born. Two days later he left 609 to become an instructor. He also took the time to write his now famous little book.

*

David Crook was destined to remain an instructor for the rest of the war. Following a course at the Central Flying School he was posted to No 15 EFTS at Carlisle, commanding A Flight, where he remained until April 1944. He then flew with two AFU's, firstly at Wheaton Aston, in Staffordshire until July, then at Ternhill until September. Going to No 41 Operational Training Unit at RAF Hawarden, near Chester, he then went to No 8 (Coastal) OTU at Dyce on 1 December 1944, having by this time amassed nearly 1660 flying hours.

Eighteen days later, Crook now thirty years of age, took-off in a Spitfire IX (EN662) to fly a mid-morning High Level Photographic sortie. At 10.52 am 13 Group Headquarters reported to RAF Dyce that a Spitfire had been seen to dive into the sea near Aberdeen from a height of 20,000 feet. A Mosquito, some Spitfires and Air Sea Rescue launches, all searched the area, but only some flying clothing was found which was identified as David's but he was not found. The Spitfire Pilot had flown his last.

5

Victor

One of the greatest RAF personalities to emerge from World War Two, and one who flew during the Battle of Britain, had, strictly speaking, no need to be a combat pilot at all. At thirty-seven years of age, and holding a Wing Commander's rank as a Station Commander, he was not supposed to even be in the air, let alone be constantly in the forefront of the battle. Not that he was a man to let that bit of officialdom deter him. His name was Victor Beamish.

Francis Victor Beamish, one of four brothers to serve with the Royal Air Force, was born in Dunmanway, County Cork, on 27 September, 1903. Completing his education at Coleraine School, he joined the RAF, entering Cranwell, from where he passed-out in August 1923. He served in England and in India, then at the Central Flying School before becoming a fighting instructor at RAF Sealand and later holding the same important post back at RAF Cranwell. In 1929 he went to Canada to help form the nucleus of fighter squadrons within the Royal Canadian Air Force. Then in 1931 he returned to England to take a post as flight commander with 25 Fighter Squadron, but shortly afterwards his flying career seemed shattered when he contracted tuberculosis and was invalided out of the service he loved so much.

With the determination that was later to make him an outstanding leader and air fighter, he decided to return to the clear open air of Canada. He took the outdoor life of a lumberjack and it was his working in this healthy active life which eventually brought about a spectacular cure which enabled him not only to rejoin the RAF three years later but to continue flying. He immediately spent a year with the RAF's Meteorological Flight, receiving the Air Force Cross for his valuable work. He was then given command of No 64 Fighter Squadron before being selected to attend the RAF Staff College at Andover. When the Second World War began he was in command of another fighter unit, 504

Squadron, but in early 1940 he was sent again to Canada and promoted to Wing Commander. Upon his return a few months later he was given command of a fighter station, RAF North Weald.

It would have been very easy for him to have remained plain Wing Commander F.V. Beamish AFC and encourage the squadrons and the pilots of his Station to great endeavours from the ground. But this was not his way at all. A born leader, an exceptional pilot, whose sheer physical presence could inspire all those under him, he was admired, well liked and revered by all ranks. Such a man could only lead from the air, lead by example. He also had a burning desire to rid the world of the Nazi regime, defeat Germany and end the war. He was exceptionally fit. In addition to his outdoor life as a lumberjack, he excelled at sport and in his earlier days had represented the RAF at Rugby and was a reserve for the Ireland team on several occasions. He would often run round the airfield after the working day rather than take an evening meal.

At North Weald there were two Hurricane fighter squadrons, 56, commanded by Squadron Leader G.A.L. Manton, and 151, led by Squadron Leader E.M. 'Teddy' Donaldson DSO. From the very first it became quite normal for Beamish to be ready for action and whenever 'his boys' went off he too took-off, either with them or to catch them up shortly afterwards. Quite often he would fly alone to watch the proceedings or join in any action, or just find his own trouble and wade in, guns blazing. This obviously put him in a very vulnerable and often dangerous position, 'easy-meat' for Me109s just looking for the opportunity to pounce on a loner or a would-be straggler. The mere fact that Victor Beamish not only survived in the often dangerous skies over southern England throughout the battle but inflicted a considerable amount of damage on the Luftwaffe, speaks volumes for his personal prowess in spite of his age.

*

His first recorded action came on 18 June 1940. In the late afternoon, 151 Squadron escorted some Blenheim bombers, flying out towards Cherbourg. As the bombers returned, 151 patrolled near the French coast and found three Heinkel 111s escorted by six Messerschmitt 109s. Considerable anti-aircraft fire was coming up at the Hurricanes but 151 climbed higher and attacked the rear bomber. Beamish went in close, sighted at the fuselage, then fired, also firing at each of the bomber's engines in turn. One engine burst into smoke and flame, then the Heinkel dived, with its undercarriage dropped. All the bombers jettisoned their bombs and flew off. Beamish was credited with a 'damaged'. He had fired a 5½ second burst and later reported that he felt that the Heinkel had been heavily armoured as he had closed right to point blank range; always the sign of a good fighter pilot. Unless a fighter pilot was an exceptional shot and could judge deflection accurately, the great air fighters used their flying skill to get in close from where their possibly average gunnery couldn't miss.

On the last day of June, 151 and 56 Squadrons again escorted Blenheims, flying at 15,000 feet. At approximately 2.45 pm, six Me109s attacked the bombers who were flying 5,000 feet below the Hurricanes. Beamish saw them and winged over to dive with 151 Squadron. He opened fire at one Messerschmitt which immediately disintegrated. Turning towards another, his fire brought smoke from its fuselage and both wings. The 109 nosed down and crashed into the sea. Again he had got in close, firing from 200 yards down to 50 yards. The first 109 had received a five-second burst, the second one ten seconds. Squadron Leader Donaldson was not so luck, being shot down, but he was rescued unhurt a short while later.

When the Battle of Britain began (officially) in July, and the Channel battles began, the North Weald squadrons were well to the fore. Shortly after 4 pm on the 9th, 151 Squadron were above a convoy off Margate at 11,000 feet when control warned them of approaching hostile aircraft. Moments later Beamish saw what he estimated as being sixty German aeroplanes, made up of twenty Ju88 and He111s, with forty Me109s and 110s. 151 Squadron went after a group of 110s who immediately formed a defensive circle. Beamish picked on one, putting a long burst into it, seeing his bullets smashing into the target but with now so many aircraft milling about him he was unable to see what happened to it. 151 Squadron reformed into line astern and made another concentrated attack; then, still having some ammunition left, Beamish circled the convoy in case further enemy aircraft came over but soon he had to retire when his petrol began to run low. Me110s were also damaged by Flying Officer A.D. Forster and Pilot Officer J.R. Hamer. One was seen to dive towards the sea by Midshipman O.M. Witeman (a Fleet Air Arm pilot attached to 151

Squadron) and apparently one Me110 of III/ZG26 was lost at approximately this time, but who exactly got it is uncertain.

Three days later, Friday the 12th, there was a tremendous battle over the Channel convoy code-named 'Booty', involving 17, 85, 242 and 151 Squadrons. Raiding Heinkel 111s and Dornier 17s of KG2 and KG53 were reported approaching soon after 8.30 am, and combat was joined by 17 Squadron at 8.48. It was well past 9 am when 151 Squadron arrived on the scene, where they found three Dorniers at 7,000 feet, twenty to thirty miles east of Orfordness.

Beamish went into the attack with the leading section. Squadron Leader Donaldson was hit by accurate return fire from the bombers, and his aircraft was severely damaged. Flying Officer J.H.L. Allan, from New Zealand, was also hit by the crossfire and was last seen heading towards the water with a dead engine. Beamish followed Donaldson's attack, also meeting accurate return fire, tracer zipping past him. He aimed at the left-hand Dornier and blew its port engine to pieces; its propeller jerked to a halt. The bomber's wheels dropped down as it broke away from the formation badly crippled. Breaking away himself, Beamish turned his attentions on the leading Dornier. His ammunition was almost spent but he kept his thumb down, firing into the port engine of the Dornier until his guns emptied. Other pilots took it in turns to attack this Dornier until it eventually ploughed into the sea soon after it had turned in an attempt to get to the English coast.

Beamish remarked in his combat report of the excellent formation kept by the German pilots, and also of the accurate return fire which not only shot down Allan, and damaged Donaldson's aeroplane (he made a splendid job of bringing his machine back to Martlesham), but also hit Beamish's Hurricane. It sustained hits in its tail, oil tank, oil lines, main spar and port wing, being rated Category 2 damage.

On 23 July came the award to Beamish of the Distinguished Service Order, the citation mentioning four victories and '... outstanding leadership and high courage have inspired all those under his command ...'

*

His next combat took place on 18 August at 5.50 pm during an attack against raiders between Chelmsford and Blackwater. He led

Blue Section of 151 Squadron when ordered off to patrol base at 10,000 feet. After some minutes the fighter controller informed the squadron that enemy aircraft were approaching from the direction of Chelmsford. Turning to intercept, they found the enemy in three distinct formations. The first consisted of thirty Me110s at 8,000 feet. A mile or so to the rear and higher up were about fifty Junkers 88s and Heinkel 111s, and again a mile or so behind these and still higher flew more menacing Me110 fighters.

In the ensuing battle, Beamish initially attacked a 110 as he dived right through the German formation but saw no visible results of his fire. Breaking away he climbed to attack a Ju88, getting in three long bursts until his guns fell silent. Smoke poured from the starboard side of it and it immediately dropped down and below the formation. Beamish was in no position to hang around, and so he broke downwards and away but he considered it probable that the 88 was a total loss. His own Hurricane (P3871) had been hit by return fire from the 88 formation, hitting both fuel tanks. Landing back at RAF North Weald, he immediately clambered into another Hurricane and returned to the scene of the fighting but the sky was clear and strangely empty.

One-five-one Squadron suffered two casualties on the 18th; its new commanding officer Squadron Leader J.A.G. Gordon (P3940) who had taken over from Donaldson on 5 August, was shot down and burned, and Pilot Officer J.B. Ramsey was killed (R4181).

On the 24th, Beamish led Red Section of 151 at 4 pm east of North Weald at 15,000 feet, finding thirty to fifty Dornier 17s escorted by a hundred or more Me110s. The bombers were packed together in close formation, the Messerschmitts circling above in the sun. Beamish went down onto a Dornier, a long burst producing smoke from the starboard side but then several 110s came screaming down to the rescue. Turning in tight circles with these 110s, Beamish heaved his fighter round in a tight merry-go-round with these 110s finally getting in a long burst at one as it drifted into his gun-sights. He saw his bullets go right into the 110 but he did not see any serious damage result. Extricating himself and now out of ammunition he went home.

His last combat during August came on the 30th, while flying with 56 Squadron when he shot up another 110, claiming it as probably destroyed.

He took-off alone on 6 September at 6 pm, behind 249 Squadron who had relieved 151 at North Weald. Climbing hard, he reached 15,000 feet and saw 249 Squadron high above him; looking down, however, he saw eight aircraft coloured black with a white stripe encircling the wings. Beamish dived and identified the aircraft as Ju87s – the infamous Stukas. As he closed in his machine was hit by return fire, but undeterred he hammered at one Stuka which burst into flames and smoke and spun away. Beamish slipped in behind another dive-bomber, fired another long burst into it, and left it losing height and emitting clouds of smoke. There was smoke haze up to 10,000 feet and as the German dive-bombers just remained in it, they had successfully evaded the British fighters flying higher up. They had in fact just attacked Thames Haven, coming in from the west. As Beamish looked down he could see Thames Haven burning in three places.

On the 11th he was flying with 249 in the late afternoon, flying at 17,000 feet south of London, when they intercepted sixty to eighty He111s which were making for London's dockland. 249 Squadron went down at them, making a semi-head-on attack although hindered by 'friendly' anti-aircraft gun fire. In consequence the squadron was broken up and Beamish climbed above the mêlée to gain a more favourable position from which to attack. Although still amid exploding AA shells, he spotted a Heinkel, swooped down, got in close and opened fire. After his last burst the Heinkel staggered and began to lose height, away and behind the rest of the bomber formation. Pilot Officer H.J.S. Beazley saw it going down and confirmed Beamish's estimate that it was finished. Five Me109s then appeared but without ammunition rightly decided not to mix it with these boys, so they half-rolled, dived down and flew home.

South of Sheppey on the 18th, having scrambled with 249 Squadron shortly before 10 am, Beamish encountered twenty to thirty Me109s at 15,000 feet. 249 was 6,000 feet higher, being vectored into another raid, but the opportunity to bounce them was too good to miss. The Messerschmitts were hard to discern, being well camouflaged; it looked very similar to British camouflage but the square wing-tips were very noticeable and at closer range the black Germanic crosses stood out plainly.

Beamish and the others dived on the 109s which were flying in open vic formations. The wing commander attacked the rearmost 109, firing two bursts into it, whereupon its wheels flopped down uselessly, a good deal of smoke poured out, and, watched by Pilot Officer P.R.F. Burton, the 109 began to go down. Burton watched it to within a few feet of the ground. Beamish, meanwhile, got in another good burst at a second Messerschmitt but three others set upon him. Again low on ammunition he decided to extricate himself so after circling with his antagonists for a short while, broke away quickly when the opportunity arose.

It was nearly a month before Beamish met 109s again, on 12 October. He now led 46 and 257 Squadrons at his station and it was while flying with them in the late afternoon of the 12th, south of London's docks, that action occurred. In fact Beamish was flying 8,000 feet above the two squadrons, at 23,000 feet, keeping his usual eye out for 'his boys'. Then he spotted more than two dozen Me109s flying in a big fan formation travelling from east to west at about 20,000 feet. On an apparent order from the 109 leader, all the Messerschmitts dropped the bombs they were carrying simultaneously.

Beamish continued to fly at the same level in the hope of breaking up the enemy formation and forcing them down to the level of 46 and 257 Squadrons. He dived finally, making a head-on pass at the formation leader. He opened fire at 300 yards, firing continuously whilst closing to about 20 yards. Black smoke poured out of the 109 which turned onto its back to dive vertically. Pulling out of his attack, Beamish turned onto the rear of the formation, making another attacking pass on the 109s, selecting one at which he commenced firing at 200 yards, closing to point blank range, but he saw no result. Then again his guns were empty.

As we have already seen, the autumn battles were particularly dangerous. This was no less true for the North Weald squadrons, or other units, Spitfire or Hurricane flown. Each tried to come to grips with the elusive bomb-carrying Messerschmitts now that the British skies were too dangerous for daylight bombing by twin-engined Heinkels, Junkers or Dorniers. And of course, these 109s were twice as dangerous once they had released their bombs. Mostly the 109s proved to be above them, sometimes but rarely they were below. However, Beamish found them below and vulnerable on 25 October, south-east of London at around 1.30 in the afternoon.

He was flying with 257 Squadron when they ran into more than fifteen Me109s below, flying in a wide vic. Leaving the outside Messerschmitts to the CO of 257 Squadron, Beamish attacked the 109 in the middle of the starboard side of the vic. Closing on it from slightly above, he fired two bursts at close range. His first burst was fired from the beam with deflection. The 109 belched smoke, turned over onto its back and fell out of formation. It spun down out of control with every sign of being destroyed. Beamish then found himself surrounded by very hostile Messerschmitts at 20,000 feet over London. He immediately went at one which flew in front of his Hurricane, letting go two good bursts which produced smoke from it as it too fell away. As he made this second attack two 109s flew on either side of his aeroplane but made no attempt to engage him. Left alone suddenly he was able to half-roll and dive to renew his attack on the 109. He chased it towards the coast at Dover, firing from astern as the 109 continued to lose height, trailing smoke and heading for a lower cloud layer. The two fighters flashed over the coast, Beamish still behind but then he spotted about 20 Messerschmitts above, so believing the 109 finished anyway, he broke off the chase and turned for home.

There was another fight with Messerschmitts on the 30th, when flying with 17 and 249 Squadrons. They saw the 109s at 23,000 feet south of London at 4.20 in the afternoon. The 109s were in layers and others could be seen at 30,000 feet. In all, Beamish estimated there were no less than two hundred Messerschmitt fighters   a formidable force! When the clash with the lower formation came, Beamish attacked two 109s in quick succession, snapping off quick bursts only. Flying south-eastwards towards the Dover area and the coast, Beamish found a pair of 109s above and ahead of him. He chased after them, attacking the outer one, giving it a long burst at fairly close range. He emptied his guns at the 109 as it dived down from 20,000 to 8,000 feet. It began to stream out coolant and it looked out of the battle but the German pilot's pals came to his rescue in the shape of six Me109s which set about Beamish when the Irishman was down to 2,000 feet above the Channel. Always seeming to be able to get out of trouble, he made a quick escape and flew home.

*

The action continued as the winter drew on and there was one

Victor Beamish seated in an American P40 Tomahawk, shares a joke with Squadron Leader Ian Gleed, CO of 87 Squadron. Beamish has just flown a mock combat with Gleed, who flew a Hurricane, to test the P40's capabilities. Colerne, 6 February, 1941.

Pilots of 249 Squadron, part of Beamish's command at North Weald.

rather special day in November when the Italian Air Force showed its face over Suffolk, North Weald's back-yard!

At around 1.30 pm, Essex radar picked up a force of hostiles approaching Harwich which led to 17, 46, 249 and 257 Squadrons being ordered into the air. Not long after 46 took-off, but before 249 were away, Victor Beamish took-off alone. The weather was rather misty so Beamish flew directly for the coast to cover convoys east of Southwold. He flew up and down the landward side of the ships and saw a large bomb explode on the water east of Harwich. Turning to investigate he came upon a dog-fight between Hurricanes and enemy aircraft. Above this he spotted two Italian Fiat CR42 biplane fighters, scrapping with a Spitfire. As he watched he saw the Spitfire half-roll very low down, and thought it was going into the sea.

The two Fiats then proceeded out to sea, flying due east. Beamish followed, caught them up and opened fire on the rear one, giving it his usual long burst from below and astern from 100 yards. His bullets raked the Fiat and it started to swing to one side. Beamish broke downwards slightly then came in again to 100 yards and fired another three-second burst. It half-rolled, began to smoke and dived vertically into a layer of haze above the water. Beamish imagined it must have gone straight in and circled to look for the other Fiat but it was long gone. Commenting later on the CR42, Beamish recorded that the paintwork on the machine looked very old and also that although it had seemed very slow in flight it could turn inside a Hurricane.

Two days later it was back to the Messerschmitts off Dover, shortly before mid-day. Beamish was on patrol with 46 and 249 Squadrons at 17,000 feet. There was a layer of very thin cloud between 14,000 and 19,000 feet that had to be watched. Drifting away on his own, Beamish lost height to around 10,000 feet, then, ten miles north-east of Dover he was pounced on by Messerschmitts from above. His first glimpse of them came in his rear-view mirror; the leading 109 was already firing, its guns flashing and sparkling. Two bullets passed right through his cockpit. Beamish hauled his machine round in a tight turn but was immediately set upon by more 109's from above; in all about twenty Me109s were milling about him. The Irishman took vigorous evasive action as he tried desperately to get away and down. His prowess as a fighter pilot was really tested and he not only got away but was able to put two good bursts into one Messerschmitt. This one broke down below the others and did not climb up again. He also fired at other 109s as they flashed in front of him but could not await results. He finally got down to sea level where the 109s left him and flew off towards Calais.

This was his last successful combat in 1940. In addition to the DSO he also received the Distinguished Flying Cross and had accounted for six German aircraft for certain. In addition he had probably destroyed or damaged at least a further fifteen. Those who knew him and who flew with him were constantly warning him of the dangers of flying alone but he always shrugged off the dangers with his disarming smile and allaying their fears with his soft Irish brogue. After all, he had proved to himself and to others that he could survive. Bob Tuck, the mercurial CO of 257 Squadron, always tried to emulate Beamish which says volumes in itself. Tuck always tried to sort out a problem by asking himself what Victor would do and that usually solved the problem.

Beamish had a terrific memory which enabled him to know every pilot and every airman's name, often knowing where they hailed from and what job they had done in peacetime. He was ruthless with those who he felt could not keep up or who were showing less warlike attitudes than he thought they should. On one occasion he had the pilots of one squadron assembled in the billiards room of the mess and made it quite clear that he would be watching and if he thought any pilot was breaking off or lagging behind for no good reason he would be after that pilot himself. They all knew what that meant, and they knew too that it was no idle threat. There was no further trouble after that, for the mere sight of Beamish's Hurricane flying off to one side or high above to the rear was more than enough to remind everyone of what he had said.

There is, of course, the often told story of when he visited a squadron and parked his machine in the place usually reserved for the squadron CO. As Beamish invariably wore an old pair of blue mechanic's overalls over his uniform without any badges of rank showing, an outraged fitter gave vent to his feelings thinking that Beamish was some idiot NCO-pilot. Saying nothing, Beamish stepped down from the aeroplane, stripped off his overalls to reveal his rank and the row of impressive decorations, handing the garment to one astonished airman! He kept promising to wear something more fitting to his rank.

One pilot who had flown with Beamish during the latter part of the Battle of Britain was Flying Officer T.F. 'Ginger' Neil DFC of 249 Squadron. He recalls the Wing Commander vividly and had cause to remember one particular sortie, flown on 13 November 1940.

'I met Victor Beamish in September 1940. He was the station commander at North Weald. Despite the fact that he had returned to the Air Force after a long bout of TB, I never saw him wear a coat or service dress hat; he was always to be seen in all sorts of weather in his tunic and side cap and, indeed, until he visited Duxford with me in the latter part of 1940 in order to attend an investiture, I don't believe I ever saw him formally dressed.

'If you flew and fought you were Victor's personal friend, regardless of rank, and you could say and do more or less what you liked. If in his view you shirked your responsibilities or didn't measure up in any way, then it was in your best interest to disappear and disappear and quickly at that. I once saw him confront a brand new officer who had just been posted to our squadron, who happened to walk into the dispersal hut a matter of moments after the rest of us had landed from a sortie. This particular young man was absolutely new; he had never so much as flown with us and unhappily for him he was from an Auxiliary Squadron and dressed accordingly with a blue non-regulation tie and a coloured lining to his uniform and coat. Victor hated him on sight, roundly reprimanded him for his dress and when the youth made some wet, but quite innocuous remark about it being 'a fad', he was ordered off the squadron and the station there and then, never to be seen again.

'Victor Beamish walked or ran everywhere except when it was necessary to get to his aircraft quickly in which case he used his Humber car. He used to have a radio in his office in station headquarters and very often knew what was going on before we did at dispersal. Sometimes, the first we knew of an approaching flight was when there was a shriek of tyres outside the dispersal hut and Victor would go leaping from his car to his aeroplane. Again, very often in the morning when we were creeping about dispersal in what I can only describe as a semi-comatose state, he would go trotting by on the perimeter track in shorts and singlet and this in the middle of winter. We once arranged a soccer match between 249 and 56 Squadrons and Victor took part. He was of course a rugger man of considerable reputation and did not have much skill at soccer but he ran about like a demented hen until most of us were exhausted not only by exertion by also by laughter. Then, because 56 Squadron were winning and he was on our side, he became very short-tempered and abusive calling us "a clapped out set of bloody ducks!"

'We also had a number of Victor's southern Irish neighbours on the airfield erecting blast walls. Whenever there was a hint of a flap they would disappear down the bomb shelters and play cards, usually for the rest of the day! Either that, or they would take to the woods or stream out through the front gate. I once saw Victor Beamish confront one of these louts, say something to him, then land a punch on the man's jaw absolutely knocking him cold. When the air raid sirens went and they streamed out of the gate, he would rush out of his office and confront them shouting abuse and grabbing them by the scruff of the neck. I am bound to say it never did very much good.

'On the flying side, Victor Beamish flew one of our aircraft which had the code letters GN-B and he used to take off with us whenever he could, or take off after us if he was a little late, and catch us up in the air. This was always a bit of a problem because he used to insinuate himself into our formation and we never knew whether we were flying twelve or thirteen. This was very undesirable as the Germans had a habit of joining formation with our squadrons every now and then in order to pick off the chaps at the back. So one spent a lot of time counting up in the air and I need hardly say that if suddenly there were thirteen rather than twelve, swift action followed.

'Another of Victor's constant tricks was to leave the formation when he heard something more exciting happening in another part of the sky. We, of course, were obliged to do what we were told, within certain limits, but Victor was always a law unto himself and he flew to where the action was. Time and time again he would come back with his aircraft peppered having run into all sorts of enemy activity usually on his own. He was a fearless fighter pilot; I have never known anybody so aggressive in the air.

'Even so, he really was a menace. Besides coming and going when he liked he knew no rules when it came to landing. Very often we used to get back to North Weald short of fuel in very miserable weather conditions to find that Victor would cut us out on the final approach and land twenty to thirty yards in front of us. This was the most irritating and aggravating aspect of the man; he was so utterly devoted to destroying the enemy that he didn't give a thought for anyone else in the air. As a result, he came very close to being shot down himself because we all flew with loaded guns and there were many times when I came within an ace of shooting at him just to teach him a lesson. When such occasions arose, once in dispersal we would go for him tooth and nail but he would be so utterly disarming in his wonderful Irish brogue, apologising and grinning all over his face, that we would finish up thinking what a wonderful chap he was.

'Like many officers of his type and kind, Victor's interest was wholly in the Royal Air Force; he didn't seem to be attracted to women at all although I'm bound to say he used to accompany us on some pretty wild benders in London. I recall on one such occasion him getting very noisy in the Dorchester Hotel and throwing dustbins down the lift shaft from the top floor. And believe you me it did not go down terribly well with the Duchesses. I remember he never referred to ladies other than by the term 'sweetie' and I never ever saw him with a sweetie of his own.

'Victor was also utterly agin the press and abhorred publicity of any sort. When we attended an investiture at Duxford, we were set upon by the press but, much to my dismay as I wanted something to show my Mum, Victor insisted that no photographs were taken of our little group with the result that now there are a large number of official photographs of my brother officers being greeted and decorated by the King and Queen and the two Princesses, but none of Victor and myself.

'In the first three weeks of September 1940 we were all under pretty heavy pressure flying up to five times a day. When we were not flying we were sleeping and occasionally eating. Victor would come round every morning when there was a break and give us a brief resumé of how he saw the battle. Like most participants in any fight we were not too concerned with the outcome but very much preoccupied with the business of fighting. There was a threat of invasion of course but I don't think that the real seriousness of the situation ever dawned on us. Victor, who knew rather more about it than we did would come in rubbing his hands and say, "They'll invade tomorrow," and when they didn't invade he was genuinely disappointed. I can hear him now saying, "Ginger, by God, I wish they'd invade."

'Needless to say I didn't altogether share his enthusiasm.

'On the 13 November 1940 we had a very unusual day. We were called out very early in the morning; it was a fine day but we had had a lot of rain over the previous several days. As we were rushing out to the other side of the airfield in order to turn into wind and take off, my aircraft fell down a hole which appeared as though by magic under my wheels and I went over with a terrible crack, and broke the propeller and tore out the engine and was left hanging down rather unpleasantly. A little later in the day, about noon time, we took off again and after wandering round at about 20,000 feet following a series of conflicting instructions, we were suddenly ordered down to 4,000 feet to attack a formation of Ju87s and 109s bombing a convoy in the Thames.

'Down we tumbled and got involved in a very exciting battle which resulted in about six of the enemy being shot down. After lunch we had a couple of hours break, then in the late afternoon we took off again, this time to patrol the Maidstone-Canterbury patrol lines. This we did quite frequently as it was a means whereby control got us airborne and in position of expectation of an enemy raid. On this particular occasion, Victor was flying with us as the fourth aircraft in the first box. As I was the senior flight commander I was the leader of the second box of four, flying straight behind him.

'In this manner we climbed up and began to patrol as instructed. There was a lot of activity further south but nothing appeared to be coming our way and I suppose we had flown up and down for the best part of three quarters of an hour, when Victor Beamish decided he was tired of doing this and he just pulled up out of formation and disappeared. As this was nothing unusual and as there was then a hole in the middle of our formation I moved up to take his place and we continued. I daresay we had been going for another quarter of an hour and I remember I was getting a bit sleepy as it was fairly late in the afternoon and we had done a fair amount that day, when suddenly there was a catastrophic bang at the back end and a terrible grinding noise.

'My aeroplane immediately stood on its tail and went vertically upwards without my knowing quite what had happened; for a moment I thought we had been attacked and I had been hit but then I realised that this could not be so. Anyway, I was far too preoccupied trying to right an aeroplane which refused to be righted and after losing flying speed it just toppled over on to its back and began to spin down with me being thrown about very unpleasantly. As we had been patrolling at about 18,000 feet I knew I had a fair amount of time and space to rectify the situation but I had no success. After spinning down for some time I suddenly found myself going through cloud which I recollected was at 6,000 feet. At that particular point I heard one of my colleagues way up in the heavens say, "I think Ginger has had it," and that had the effect of needling me into action.

'I then started to get out and after a good deal of difficulty managed to leave the cockpit bumping my head very nastily on the wing. After freeing myself from the aeroplane, everything worked as it should and I found myself floating down at about 1,500 feet over a pretty substantial wood. I then fell into the trees and promptly fell out of one of the tallest of them after which I remember nothing until I awoke to find a series of feet around me and a rather agitated discussion going on as to whether I was a German and alive or dead. I was able to reassure them that I was not a German and very much alive, but I was unable to stand and eventually had to be carried some way, finishing up at an army post where I was given some tea and was able to have a bath. Apart from damaging my leg I was otherwise in good shape but I could not get through on the telephone to North Weald and it was not until some hours later that they learned I was still alive; indeed they had written me off and were almost packing my kit.

'I got back to North Weald late that night and was confronted by Victor Beamish who was at his most disarming. Apparently, he had left our formation, decided that there was nothing doing elsewhere and taken it upon himself to rejoin the squadron, quite overlooking the fact that I was in the place that he had vacated. When the collision occurred he lost his propeller and the front part of his engine but at least his aeroplane was flyable and he managed to control it and glide to land on Detling airfield which was not too far away. He was full of remorse, full of Irish blarney, and I almost finished up apologising to *him* for the collision.

'Victor flew with us constantly throughout the winter of 1940 and then in the spring of 1941 he was posted away and was replaced by Wing Commander Vincent. (Later Air Vice-Marshal S.F. Vincent CB DFC AFC, he had been a fighter pilot in the First World War and also in 1940.) Vincent was an entirely different type of man, much quieter, very effective in his own way but certainly not a Victor Beamish.

'Before Victor left, I recall having a rather heated conversation with him after we had completed a rather difficult sortie over France. At this stage we were having a thin time of it because the Huns had just been re-equipped with the 109F which had a considerably better performance than our Hurricanes and we were very much on the receiving end. I remember in a fit of excitement and disappointment saying to Victor that we were sitting ducks in Hurricanes and how I wished we could go to the Western Desert, anywhere other than stooging over France escorting bombers and getting shot at. I never gave it another thought but a month or so later Victor turned up and said that he had news for us; he had spoken for us in the right quarter and we were going to be posted to the Middle East. (The moral to this particular story is when under stress say nothing, for fear of getting something worse – we ended up in Malta!)

'As a result of this casual conversation with Victor Beamish, 249 Squadron were indeed posted to the Middle East and I went with them. They remained there throughout the war, finishing as the highest scoring squadron in the RAF; a very considerable record.

'I came back from the Middle East in the spring of 1942 and by this time Victor was Group Captain at Biggin Hill. I wrote to him immediately and said that when my period of penance at 81 Group was over I would like to join him. He replied at once welcoming me back, saying that he would fix it up. Unhappily this never came to pass, as shortly after his discovery of the *Scharnhorst* and *Gneisenau* in the English Channel, he was killed and that was that.

'Victor Beamish came from Northern Ireland and epitomised the northern Irish fighting man. He was absolutely without fear, a dedicated and devoted RAF officer, and the salt of the earth.'

*

Beamish continued to lead and command the North Weald squadrons in the new year of 1941, the year Fighter Command began to take the war to the Germans over northern France. The offensive reached its peak in the high summer but the first faltering steps began very early in the year, on 10 January to be precise.

Fifty-six and 249 Squadrons were part of the first fighter sweep on that January day and Victor Beamish was not going to miss being a part of it. The action, when it came, took place when the fighters were actually returning across the Channel from St Ingelvert, from what had so far proved an uneventful mission. Initially 249 Squadron spotted some German patrol boats off Calais; Beamish, never slow to hit the enemy, dived down to machine-gun them, and saw his fire rake the decks. Having regained height and when about mid-Channel, Beamish saw a Hurricane being attacked by what he thought was a Spitfire. The Hurricane was not taking any evasive action and was streaming glycol. As Beamish turned to identify the offender, he saw it had a yellow nose – it was a Messerschmitt. He was quickly after it, giving it two bursts, one a deflection shot and then the second from dead astern. The 109 hit badly, went down and crashed into the sea.

As the year progressed, Beamish, as an experienced and acknowledged air fighter, became more and more involved in the planning of these offensive operations across the Channel, but he continued to lead from the air whenever he could, often as wing leader. He flew with his North Weald wing in 9 August, escorting Blenheims against the power station at Gosnay. Shortly after crossing the coast of France an Me109F pulled up from below him and fired at his Spitfire. Beamish saw the tracer shells flash past and attacked the 109 in turn sending it down streaming glycol and black smoke. Later, over the target area he fired at another 109, blasting pieces off it and seeing it fall away smoking badly.

*

It was to be some months before the genial Irishman was to make another combat claim. In the meantime he left North Weald, received a bar to his DSO, then took command of RAF Debden, being promoted to Group Captain. Soon afterwards he took command of RAF Kenley.

Beamish continued to fly on operations and on 12 February 1942 became famous for discovering the convoy of German capital ships, *Scharnhorst*, *Gneisenau*, and *Prinz Eugen* steaming up the Channel in what became known as their 'Channel Dash'. He was out flying a Rhubarb operation with Kenley's Wing Leader, Wing Commander Finley Boyd. Looking for trouble they certainly found it when they gave chase to a couple of Me109s, only to fly into the middle of the German defences over the ships. The two pilots quickly turned tail and sped back to break the news. There followed the desperate attempts by the RAF and FAA to stop the ships, and at some cost but to little avail. Beamish flew out also in the early afternoon by which time the ships and their air and naval escort were roughly opposite Margate. With the Wing he found the ships stretched out between Mardyck and Gravelines. The most Beamish could do was to dive down to attack two destroyers, attacking one from dead astern, raking it from stem to stern despite terrific return fire.

The following morning he led 452 Australian Squadron over the Channel to see if any of the previous day's activity was still in evidence. Off Boulogne at 10.35 am they found a Heinkel 115 just above sea level, obviously looking for lost pilots from the previous day. Beamish's first burst hit the rear cockpit area which caused an explosion, pieces fell off the aircraft and burning petrol set the floats on fire. His attack was followed up by a veritable massacre by 11 Australian pilots, which ended when the Heinkel finally fell blazing into the sea.

A little less than a month later, on 9 March, he attached himself to the Kenley Wing with an independent section. 602 Squadron was flying close escort, 452 middle cover and 485 Squadron as top cover. After a rendezvous with six Bostons over Rye, the Spitfires took them to Marzingarbe. Nearing the French coast on the way out, several FW190s dived to attack the bombers. Beamish was behind the bombers as two of the Focke Wulfs got through the top cover. He went after them, catching up the second 190, his fire producing smoke as it fell away. The Wing Leader, Wing

Commander D.O. Findlay DFC, saw two FW190s crash into the sea below, one being credited to the Group Captain.

On the 14th, Beamish led the Kenley wing as escort cover to Bostons. They missed the rendezvous but carried on to the target – shipping off Le Havre. They found six E-boats with a flak ship. Ordering 452 and 602 Squadrons to stay above, Beamish led 485 down to attack the boats, the Irishman raking the rearmost E-boat, closing to 200 feet, and white smoke enveloped the vessel.

Beamish again led the wing on the afternoon of 26 March on Ramrod 17 to Le Havre with twenty-two Bostons. On the approach to Le Havre bandits were reported at 6,000 feet and then as the bombers swung into the target, twelve Me109Fs and two or three FW190s were seen up-sun. These dived to the attack and, turning, Beamish got a 190 in his sights and fired a three second burst. The 190 poured out smoke, but then a 109E presented itself and he attacked. Two pilots of 485 Squadron saw the 190 go down and explode. Beamish also hit the Messerschmitt and with his Number Two, followed it down, streaming smoke, until it was diving vertically at less than 200 feet. Then Wing Commander Boyd warned Beamish of a German fighter behind and he had to pull away. Another pilot saw the 109 go into the sea just north of the harbour.

These victories brought his total score to at least 11 destroyed, 9 probables and 8 damaged; not bad for an 'old man' of 38 who really need not have been in action at all! Yet his continued presence on operations inspired all who flew with him, especially the new, young pilots in the Wing. Unhappily his luck ran out on 28 March 1942.

Flying with the New Zealanders of 485 Squadron on a sweep, they found forty FW190s and Me109s just inland from Gris Nez, about to dive on another wing. Beamish led the Spitfires down and the squadron became split-up. With two other pilots Beamish attacked two 190s but they quickly dived away. He was then attacked by two others in quick succession and although Flight Lieutenant R.J.C. Grant, his wingman, shot down one of the assailants the other must have got the group captain. Beamish was last seen flying low over the French coast towards England but failed to make it back across the grey waters of the Channel.

6

Cowboy

Howard Peter Blatchford, who became known as 'Cowboy' Blatchford to his intimate friends, came from Edmonton, Alberta, Canada, to gain undying fame when the Italian Regia Aeronautica made their first raid against England on Armistice Day, 11 November 1940.

Blatchford came to England to join the Royal Air Force while peace still reigned in Europe, but when war did come, he was a Spitfire pilot, serving with Number 41 Squadron based at RAF Catterick. In the period now referred to as the Phoney War, between September 1939 to May 1940, which ceased abruptly when the Germans invaded the Lowlands on 10 May, the RAF had several alerts along its northern and eastern coasts. In these sometimes brief but deadly encounters, several German daylight raiders or reconnaissance aeroplanes were shot down, one falling to 41 Squadron as early as 17 October 1939..

It was in the late afternoon of that day that Cowboy Blatchford led Flight Sergeant E.A. Shipman and Sergeant Harris on a patrol over the coast at Whitby. They had been flying for some time when at about 4.30 pm Flight Sergeant Shipman saw a Heinkel 111 bomber eight to nine miles out to sea. Reporting the sighting to Blatchford, Shipman immediately peeled off and dived at the German aeroplane which quickly turned eastwards to begin a long gentle dive from its height of 10,000 feet. Its dark and effective camouflage could be plainly seen and as Shipman closed to make the first attack he could see its mud coloured tail and fuselage with green diamond shaped markings on it; what is now called splinter camouflage.

As Shipman ended his first pass, Sergeant Harris made a standard Fighter Command Number One attack, then Blatchford did likewise from dead astern and from slightly below. The Canadian's first burst from 400 yards lasted for a full ten to twelve seconds – nearly using up all his ammunition. In his eager anticipation he approached far too fast and was forced to pull up and over the Heinkel's tail in order to avoid hitting it. Hauling his Spitfire round he made his second attack at a much slower speed and firing again from 400 yards was able to hold his position without difficulty to fire the remainder of his ammunition. After both attacks, Blatchford was able to fly alongside the starboard side of the Heinkel as close as 200 yards and could clearly see the rear dorsal gun pointing uselessly into the air with no sign of a gunner (probably hit by one of the NCO pilots). Sergeant Harris came in and made another firing pass after his leader's final attack and shortly afterwards the bomber smacked down flatly on the surface of the North Sea. Blatchford and Harris flew around the machine for three or four minutes, watching as two men clambered out of the top cockpit hatch to slide down to stand on the wing. Finally the two Spitfires had to fly back to base, Blatchford reporting the location of the downed bomber over his radio, which was approximately twenty-five miles east of Whitby.

*

It was to be nearly a year before Cowboy Blatchford was to claim a further victory. In the interim he went to France to fly with 212 Squadron which was a detachment from the Photographic Development Unit. He flew with 212 until the fall of France and then continued with the PDU itself. It was not until late September 1940 that he managed to get back to a fighter squadron, being posted to 17 Squadron, flying Hawker Hurricanes; a strange posting for someone with over two years experience of flying Spitfires

He flew several sorties during the last few days of September and was flying Blue 3 to Flight Lieutenant A.W.A. Bayne shortly after 10 am on 2 October. It was similar to his first action in that they had been in the air for some time before they spotted a hostile aeroplane – a Dornier 17 – about eight miles north-east of Colchester at between 4,000 and 5,000 feet, flying in and out of 8/10ths cloud. The Hurricanes attacked, Bayne getting in a burst as well as Pilot Officer F. Fajtl, a Czech pilot. Later Pilot Officer J.K. Ross also got in an attack on it.

Blatchford saw the Dornier still flying in the clouds right below him, dived and opened fire at 400 yards. On his second attack he got in closer – 250 to 200 yards, after which the port engine of the bomber began to give out a greyish white smoke, streaking out for a distance of 200 yards or so, which lasted for several seconds. It was probably coolant draining away. Blatchford gained height to watch the enemy aircraft and saw a Hurricane make a pass at it from the left, then break away to the right.

The Dornier then dropped right into the clouds but Blatchford followed, closing to twenty yards, firing short bursts whenever he saw the grey shape of the bomber in the fluffy opaque clouds. Pieces of the aeroplane started to come off the Dornier, whizzing back and passing Blatchford's Hurricane. He could also make out a red glow in the rear of the bomber and another between the port engine and the wing root. He then pulled away to the right as they emerged from the cloud and he fired two more bursts from the starboard quarter. The Dornier made a turn but Blatchford hammered it again, his bullets smashing into the port engine again, as well as the left side of the fuselage which began to burn.

By now Blatchford's fuel state was critical. He had been on patrol for ninety minutes before the fight began and he had been chasing and firing at it in and out of cloud for some time. In fact, both Blatchford and Fajtl ran so short of petrol that both had to force land near Pulham. the Dornier, from the Staff *Staffel* of KG2, also crash-landed near Pulham, South Norfolk; its crew Oberleutnant Hans Langer, the *Staffel Kapitän*, Oberleutnant Erich Eitze, and Unteroffiziers Seidel and Bellman, were all taken prisoner. Pilot Officer Ross put down near the Dornier which was completely burnt out; only the wings and tail remained intact. The Dornier was eventually shared between Bayne, Ross, Fajtl and Blatchford.

Cowboy's next action was the famous one on 11 November. He was now A Flight commander in 257 Squadron, following the request by 257's Commanding Officer, Squadron Leader Bob Tuck, for an experienced flight commander. Much to Tuck's later regret, he was away from the squadron on the 11th and so it was Blatchford who led the squadron when a raid was reported. Leading Red Section they scrambled from their base at North Weald to patrol base at 10,000 feet before flying to the coast when ordered to do so. They met up with 17 Squadron off the coast who

(*Centre*) Cowboy Blatchford

Cowboy Blatchford climbing out of the cockpit of his Hurricane.

257 Squadron, November 1940. Seated, left to right: Peter Cowboy Blatchford, Squadron Leader Robert Stanford Tuck, and Flight Lieutenant Prosser Hanks.

were flying 8,000 feet below them and at the same time as the Controller warned 257 that enemy aircraft were approaching from the east. Blatchford later said:

> When we were about 12,000 feet I saw nine planes of a type I had never seen before, coming along in tight 'vic' formation. I didn't like to rush in bald-headed until I knew what they were, so the squadron went up above them to have a good look. Then I realised they were not British, and that was good enough for me.

He continued:

> I must say that the Italians, as they turned out to be, stood up to it very well. They kept their tight formation and were making for the thick cloud cover at 20,000 feet, but our tactics were to break them up before they could do that and we succeeded.

The bombers which the Canadian thought were either Caproni 135s or Fiat BR20s, were flying NWN on his port side. Having satisfied himself that they were indeed hostile, he led the squadron down for a beam attack.

> I selected near starboard bomber and opened with a beam attack firing a four-second burst. I observed no apparent result. I passed over the port side and did a quarter attack on the rearmost port bomber. Owing to my speed I repeated the same attack with a two-second burst. Bomber then looped violently and went into a vertical dive towards the sea and disintegrated before hitting the sea.

Blatchford guessed he must have killed the pilot who had pulled back on his control column thus putting his machine into a loop. As the Fiat tumbled towards the sea it began to break up into hundreds of small pieces, or as he described it, 'falling to the sea like a snowstorm'.

He then attempted to get at the bombers again but then saw a large formation of antiquated biplane fighters, Fiat CR42s. He climbed up behind one but its pilot saw him coming, turned towards him and began quite a dog-fight. He discovered the CR42 to be a very nimble adversary but finally his shots registered. The Fiat waffled extensively and lost height. Other Fiats engaged the Canadian and another dog-fight developed but this time Blatchford's eight guns were silent – he was out of ammunition. He found another CR42 ahead of him, about 30 yards, and he was just a few feet above it as he closed.

> At that moment I decided that as I could not shoot him down I would try and knock him out of the sky with my aeroplane. I went kind of haywire. It suddenly occurred to me what a good idea it would be to scare the living daylights out of him. I aimed for the centre of his top mainplane, did a quick dive and pulled out just before crashing into him. I felt a very slight bump, but I never saw him again and somehow I don't think he got back.

Although he lost nine inches off two of his propeller blades which set up a certain amount of vibration he assisted another Hurricane who was scrapping with three CR42s. He made a dummy head-on attack on two, and the Italian pilots immediately headed out to sea.

On landing he found that his propeller was, in addition to the damage, splashed with blood. The Italians lost three BR20s and three CR42s. 46 Squadron who were also engaged in this action, and 257, claimed a total of 14 Italian aeroplanes shot down, so clearly there was a good deal of over-claiming. In reality everyone was taking pot shots as targets presented themselves and everyone thought it had been his own fire that had inflicted the vital damage. There was even some suggestion that a pilot of 46 Squadron had fired into Blatchford's BR20 as it dived towards the sea and made a part claim.

Whatever the result, and whether in fact Blatchford's propeller had given his CR42 pilot more than a scratch!, his leadership and the fact that he aggressively rammed his opponent, brought Cowboy Blatchford the award of the Distinguished Flying Cross for his part in the action. He and his exploit became widely known and several dramatic pictures and drawings of his famous ramming found their way into aviation magazines and history books of the war. His CO, not unnaturally, was peeved at being away and missing all the fun. He, (Tuck) and Blatchford later went to inspect the wreck of one BR20 which had crashed at Tangham Forest,

Bromeswell, being astounded by the equipment which they found in the bomber, including tin helmets, bayonets as well as a goodly supply of food and wine, everything, it seemed the men of Mussolini's Air Force needed while engaged on operations.

*

Ever since Blatchford arrived on Tuck's squadron, the two men had become firm friends. Blatchford would call Tuck 'boss', or 'Bobbie' but hardly ever the more formal title of 'Sir'! Sometimes it was even 'Beaky' referring to Tuck's long nose. Blatchford in turn was sometimes Pete or Peter, then Cowboy – and sometimes 'Fat Arse'! The Canadian had two main interests when not flying, Hill-Billy music and women. The former was harmless, but on one occasion Tuck had to rescue his friend from an irate army officer who had discovered Blatchford with the man's wife, having to talk the officer into putting down a revolver he was pointing towards the slightly inebriated, smiling and certainly unrepentant Canadian.

*

Less than a week after the Italian raid, on 17 November, Blatchford was again leading the squadron on a convoy patrol, being airborne at 8.48 am. Being vectored to fly on a course of 190° and flying south-east of Harwich, he saw a number of Messerschmitt 109 fighters in no set formation, flying south-south-west at 8,000 feet. He led the Hurricanes up into the sun, endeavouring to cut off the 109s who were now on his starboard side. As the two groups converged, the 109 pilots realised that the Hurricanes held the advantage, made a left turn towards them, forcing the RAF boys to attack from head-on. Cowboy opened fire on the leading 109 at about 300 yards with a four-second burst. Immediately he began firing, so did the 109 pilot. Closing quickly the German broke away and over the top of the Canadian's machine and as he went, Blatchford gave it a short deflection shot, then pulled the Hurricane round in a tight right-hand turn. Levelling out he saw that his fire had inflicted some damage, for the Messerschmitt now ahead of him was streaming black smoke from the engine area. The 109 went into a right hand turn downwards and as Blatchford closed in another Hurricane crossed in front of the German. He watched helplessly as the German, although hit badly, fired a burst into the Hurricane which immediately spewed out a stream of coolant before falling away in a controlled spin.

Blatchford engaged the 109 again, from dead astern, firing from behind and above. At 1,500 feet the 109 flattened out of its dive and Blatchford put the finishing touches to it. The Messerschmitt did a cartwheel as it hit the water; the pilot was jettisoned into the sea some thirty yards ahead of his aeroplane.

*

The battle over, Cowboy Blatchford remained with 257 Squadron until well into the new year. His next successful combat came on 19 March 1941, thirty-five miles east of Southwold just before 8 pm. 257 Squadron was stationed now at Coltishall, Norfolk, and had been ordered up to provide escort for some bombers flying out over the North Sea. Reaching 15,000 feet, Control ordered Blatchford onto a course of 140° at 7.30 pm. Over the sea he saw some red lights being shot into the air from the surface but could see no sign of shipping in the failing light. This was followed shortly afterwards by a white flare which began to slowly float down. However, the Controller told him not to investigate – obviously a night-fighter was already after an intruder above a convoy.

Then Control informed him of a bandit quite near to his position and sent him westwards. He lost height to 12,000 feet – it was now nearly dark – and was informed that the raider was virtually beside him. Blatchford made a turn to the east in the hope of putting the enemy plane on his port side between him and the setting sun. Then he saw it. The bandit was just 300 yards away and Blatchford came down to its level and the German fired a three-star green and red cartridge flare. The Canadian was still on the German's dark side so was almost certainly invisible to the enemy crew. However, they were obviously suspicious, for the enemy pilot began turning to the left and then the right as if to try and see behind him. Blatchford could now make out the shape of a Ju88, and then attacked from the port quarter from 200 yards:

I could see my tracer hitting EA. Towards the end of my burst the top rear-gunner gave me a short burst and I felt a hit on my port side. However, his fire ceased before mine and immediately he began to dive and rapidly got into an almost vertical position.

I followed EA down but realised I could not continue for fear of crashing into the sea. Therefore, I pulled up and lost EA in the haze.

He circled for several minutes but saw nothing and the ground Controller informed him that the plot on the radar screen had ceased at approximately his position. He returned to base, landing at 8.30 pm, being credited with a 'probable'.

He was more successful on the night of 11/12 May at 00.14 am to be precise, ten miles north-east of Happisburgh at 6,500 feet. The previous night, of course, had seen the great London Blitz further south of Blatchford's usual patrol area. He had left Coltishall at 11.15 pm in a Hurricane Mark II, to patrol the coast from Yarmouth to Sheringham. Again after investigating some flares over the sea, he saw an aeroplane approaching from the east at 500 feet above his position. He swung round as it passed, keeping position about 300 yards below the machine which he could now see was a Heinkel, its exhaust stubs glowing in the dark. Closing in, he opened fire from 50 yards, whereupon the port engine on the Heinkel flared up. As the German machine began to lose height he gave it another burst from 150 yards, then a third burst which produced an explosion in the fuselage. A piece of the aeroplane flew back and a fire blazed on the wing between the starboard engine and the fuselage. Further attacks set the starboard engine alight and the Heinkel finally crashed into the sea.

*

In July 1941, Cowboy Blatchford took over command of 257 Squadron and he began to lead them on bomber escort missions over France to supplement its convoy and night-fighter patrol duties. Then he was given command of the Digby Wing before being rested from operations. He returned to more active duty in the spring of 1943, taking command of the Coltishall Wing on 5 February. On 18 March while escorting Ventura bombers to Maasluis in Holland, the bombers had just commenced their return journey when FW190s attacked. Blatchford dived on one firing from 200 to 100 yards and it rolled over and spun down inverted. He then attacked the leading Focke Wulf and it turned onto its back, lost a wing and the pilot baled out before the spinning

190 hit the sea.

The Wing escorted bombers against Rotterdam on 4 April, and heavy flak damaged two Venturas. Turning for England, two other Venturas began lagging behind but Blatchford took a section of Spitfires down to cover them when FW190s appeared. A fight started but they successfully defended the Vents, with Blatchford probably damaging two of the German single-seaters.

Blatchford had changed considerably since the days of 1940. He seemed much older to his friends and far more serious than he had previously been, occasionally philosophical or even cynical. Operation followed operation, sortie followed sortie – the war still had two years to run and it was a fact that the longer the former Battle of Britain heroes (they would decry that title) stayed in combat the greater the chance that their luck would desert them. As someone remarked once in a war film, one thing about being one of the Few was that as time went on they got Fewer!

Wing Commander Blatchford claimed a FW190 as probably destroyed on 2 May 1943. He was leading 118 and 167 Squadrons as escort to twelve Venturas attacking the steel works at Ijmuiden, when a battle began against eighteen Focke Wulfs.

The following afternoon he led 118, 167 and 504 Squadrons as escort to eleven Venturas, the target being a power station near Amsterdam. Three Vents were shot down over Holland and in the event, neither the bombers nor their Spitfire escort got through to the target. In total ten Venturas were lost and two of 167 Squadron's machines damaged. In a desperate air battle with enemy fighters, Blatchford's Spitfire was hit in the petrol tank and began to lose fuel. He was eventually forced to ditch into the sea some forty miles off the English coast and although rescue searches were made he was not seen again.

7

Richard

It might seem that there is little more than can be said about the one person whose name and story is synonymous with the Battle of Britain – Richard Hillary. It has virtually all been said. His own book *The Last Enemy* left us a vivid picture of his RAF life. It is a classic in every sense of the word but one which, for me, took time to appreciate and understand. Its pages fill one with both sadness and admiration; sadness because one soon realises what splendid young men were sacrificed to the god of War; admiration because one but cannot be a part of this young man's suffering, and will to survive the most appalling injuries.

In his book (published by Macmillan & Co, 1942) are expressed the feelings of dear friends being lost in much the same way that David Crook expressed his sudden loss of friends in his book; and probably only in Tom Gleave's book[1], *I Had a Row with a German* (also by Macmillan & Co, 1941) does one come into contact again with the very personal suffering that men like Gleave and Hillary experienced. An experience that no one can really imagine unless they have themselves been inside the blazing cockpit of an aeroplane watching their own flesh burning. Any one who has read *The Last Enemy*, should also endeavour to read *Richard Hillary*, a biography written by Lovat Dickson (Macmillan & Co, 1950) for this book gives yet another insight into the life of Richard Hillary. Whilst mentioning these books, one other is recommended, *Pilot's Wife's Tale* by Esther Terry Wright (The Women's Book Club, 1942) for this almost unknown book gives a wife's story whose young fighter pilot husband was shot down and badly burned.[2]

[1] Tom Gleave commanded 253 Squadron during the Battle. On 31 August 1940 he was shot down and badly burned. He later retired as a Group Captain.

[2] The subject was Pilot Officer David W. Hunt of 257 Squadron, who was shot down on 3 September – within the same hour as Richard Hillary. He too later flew again.

Richard Hope Hillary was born in Australia on 20 April 1919, his father being in the Australian Treasury in Melbourne. When Richard was three years old his father came to London to take a post with Australia House, bringing his family with him. When later his father had to work in the Sudan, Richard stayed at school in England. In 1931 Richard went to Shrewsbury Public School from where he proceeded to Oxford University in 1937, entering Trinity College as an undergraduate. He loved and enjoyed sport, being at various times, the President of the Rugby Club, secretary of the Boat Club, was at the time the University's best cricketer and also participated in golf, running and hockey. As an indication of his future fame as a writer he was editor of the university's magazine *Isis*. He took part in all the usual events of the university, being what might be termed as a typical undergraduate of the day.

With most of his friends and contemporaries, although having strong anti-war feelings, he joined the University Air Squadron, but initially for the pure delight of flying. However, he believed that, in the troubled world of the period, if war did come, at least in an aeroplane he could fight in that war as a gentleman, as a knight in shining armour rather than slogging it out in some muddy trench. When war did come, he, like most of his college chums, followed through and completed their flying training to become Royal Air Force pilots. Two of his particular pals were Noel Agazarian and Peter Howes. Agazarian was to fly alongside David Crook in 609 Squadron, do very well in the Battle of Britain and die undecorated in 1941. Peter Howes also fought in the battle, with 54, 234, and 603 Squadrons, only to die in action on 18 September. In his final training he met up with two new friends, Peter Pease and Colin Pinckney. Together these three were posted to 603 (City of Edinburgh) Squadron, commanded by Squadron Leader George Denholm. 603 Squadron was, of course, in Scotland, and so the three friends and newly fledged fighter pilots, travelled north.

Peter Pease became an influence on Richard's thinking and also a very special friend. He was also an enigma for Richard to try and understand. In their brief but hectic and exciting weeks together it is doubtful if Richard succeeded in really getting into the mind of his friend. Understanding was to come after Peter's death.

*

I began this chapter by questioning if any more could really be written about Richard Hillary. Intellectually probably not. However, to fit in with part of the theme of this book we can look a little closer at what he actually did in the battle, what he actually achieved in the summer sky over southern England.

His friend Peter Pease was the first of the trio to fire his guns in anger. Just after mid-day on 30 July he was on patrol with his flight commander, Flight Lieutenant F.W. Rushmer, and Pilot Officer R. Berry when they were ordered to orbit fifteen miles south-east of Montrose at 14,000 feet. They spotted a Heinkel 111 ahead and below, the bomber diving through some light cloud. The section attacked from behind while the Heinkel continued its dive. Then it turned westward and Pease came into range to fire two short deflection bursts into it. Pease followed up this attack and the others also fired. The bomber continued to descend, its wheels hanging down, both of its engines smoking, until it hit the sea and burst into flames.

Then came the eagerly awaited order to move south to where the battle was raging. Twenty-four pilots of the squadron flew south to RAF Hornchurch in Essex on 10 August. As Hillary recorded in his book, of those twenty-four, only eight were to fly back.

For the first few days in action, Richard was probably happy just to survive – and have the time to learn his trade. His first success came on 29 August. He was to continue in action for just six days!

The morning of the 29th was quiet but in the afternoon, radar plots came onto the screens, WAAF plotters began to place markers on large scale maps in operations rooms, and 603 Squadron was one of thirteen fighter units sent into the air to meet the threat. 603 became airborne at 3.15 pm, Hillary flying Spitfire L1021 coded XT-M, led by Squadron Leader Denholm, 'Uncle George' to his men.

Fighter Command, at this stage in the battle, were anxious not to let its valuable pilots become embroiled in dog-fights with German fighters unless bombers were in evidence. These were Keith Park's (AOC 11 Group) express orders for he could see the danger of frittering away his fighter force in combat with Messerschmitt 109s which in themselves posed no threat to England. 603 Squadron, however, made contact with Me109s near Deal and in a brief scrap one 109 was claimed as destroyed, three others probably destroyed. Richard Hillary was credited with one of the probable victories. Hillary and the squadron landed back at Hornchurch at around 5 pm although he and Colin Pinckney had to make force-landings.

It was not too serious, for Hillary was off again in L1021 at 6.10 pm. Forty minutes later they ran into two dozen Me109s over Ashford, chasing them to the coast. Hillary opened fire at one which went down on fire, being confirmed by the Royal Observer Corps as going into the sea. The fight continued but finally the 109s broke off the action to fly southwards towards France. Only then did Hillary have a moment to think of what had occurred. Later he was to write down his feelings:

It had happened. My first emotion was one of satisfaction at a job adequately done, at the final logical conclusion of months of specialised training. And then I had a feeling of the essential moment just how lucky a fighter pilot is. He has none of the personalised emotions of the soldier, handed a rifle and bayonet and told to charge. The fighter pilot's emotions are those of the duellist – cool, precise, impersonal. He is privileged to kill well. For if one must either kill or be killed, as now one must, it should, I feel, be done with dignity. Death should be given the setting it deserves; it should never be a pettiness; and for the fighter pilot it never can be.

*

Richard Hillary had no contact with the Luftwaffe on the 30th, but on the 31st he and 603 scrambled at 12.40 pm. Hillary was strapped into Spitfire X4277, again coded 'M'. As in the previous days, the Luftwaffe were after the RAF's airfields. This was not the first clash of the day, in fact it was the third, but it was the most heavy, over a hundred enemy aircraft crossing the English coast at Dungeness. One group headed for Croydon, another towards Biggin Hill. 603 Squadron found one large formation of fifty Messerschmitt 109s at 18,000 feet, escorting Dornier 17s and Heinkel 111s. They attacked and in the subsequent dog-fight, Hillary slid in behind one Messerschmitt, closed to 200 yards before opening fire, then let go a four second burst, by which time he had quickly to break away for fear of hitting his adversary. The 109 dived away and crashed into the English Channel.

He was in action again on 1 September, flying R6721 on a

scramble at 3.45 pm, but it was to be on 2 September that Hillary the fighter pilot was going to have his day, and was going to shine – albeit it was a short lived moment.

He was back in X4277, one of the new Mark II Spitfires beginning to reach the squadrons. The day began warm and hazy and the Luftwaffe, continuing its attempts at knocking out RAF fighter airfields, was up early. At 7.15 am raids were building up over Calais which eventually formed into an estimated forty bombers and sixty fighters. They came on towards North Weald, Eastchurch, Rochford and Biggin Hill aerodromes. Eleven RAF squadrons were scrambled – five making contact. 603 was up to defend its own base at Hornchurch, but when it became clear that it was not in immediate danger they were redirected onto German fighters on their way back to the Channel and home.

Hillary had been flying for twenty minutes when at 8.15 am he spotted three Me109s north of RAF Hawkinge flying at 26,000 feet. These were some of the JG51 and in the scrap which followed with several 109s, at least three, possibly four, were shot down by 603 Squadron. Hillary himself put one of them into the sea. They were back on the ground by 8.30 and the day had hardly begun.

At eight minutes past mid-day, 603 Squadron was racing into the air again. This time an estimated 250 fighters and bombers approached Dover, an armada which began to split up into groups. The RAF had seventy Hurricanes and Spitfires in the air to engage them. 603 made contact at five minutes after one o'clock, wading into part of a balbo of eighty Messerschmitt 109s. Hillary's personal combat report recorded:

> When five miles off Sheppey I saw formation of 109s. I chased one over to France and fired at it. I saw the enemy aircraft's perspex hood break up but as it was a head-on attack I was unable to see anything more of it. I then saw a squadron of Me 109s at the same height as myself, 23,000 feet, it was turning in formation. I attacked outside Me109 with three short bursts and saw it spin down emitting black and white smoke. After a few seconds it caught fire.

The squadron began landing back at 1.35 pm; Richard received credit for one Me109 destroyed and one damaged. One of 603's pilots had to make a wheels-up landing following his attack on a Dornier, but otherwise the squadron was intact.

Their third sortie of the day began just after four o'clock as another wave of 250 German aeroplanes headed in towards Dover before spreading out over the Kent countryside. Biggin Hill, Brooklands and Kenley were all targets as well as Detling, Eastchurch – and also Hornchurch. Over Hornchurch, eleven of 603's Spitfires climbed to a level of 23,000 feet, to find a huge triangle of about fifty bombers and at least the same number of fighters, loose and in vics, stepped up to 20,000 feet. Being above them the squadron was able to dive on them – then the dog-fights started. Hillary's third combat report of the day stated:

> I lost sight of the squadron and saw four Me109s in line astern above me. I climbed up and attacked rear 109, getting to about fifty feet of him before opening fire. The Me109 went straight down with thick smoke pouring out and I did not see it again.

Ten Spitfires landed back at Hornchurch around 6.20. Sergeant J. Stokoe was missing, shot down by 109s near Maidstone, wounded and forced to bale out. Hillary was credited with a probable which made his day's total two destroyed, one probably destroyed and one damaged during his three sorties on 2 September.

*

Came Tuesday 3 September; ironically for Richard Hillary, his last combat would take place on the first anniversary of the beginning of the war, almost to the hour. It was a fine warm day with a summer haze over the Channel and the Straits of Dover. By 8 am the radar plots began to identify the build-up of enemy aircraft above Calais.

At 603's dispersal, Richard Hillary was having a spot of trouble with his cockpit hood on X4277. It was not sliding along its groove properly. Hoping that an alert would not come too early, he and a fitter began working with a file and lubricating oil to get the hood sliding properly and smoothly. They eased it slightly but at 9.15 came the order to scramble. The hood was still not 100% and it was to cost the good-looking Hillary dear.

Squadron Leader Denholm led his pilots into the morning sunshine. Again it was 603's own backyard into which the

Luftwaffe was approaching, its targets being the airfields at Debden, North Weald and Hornchurch. Later, from his hospital bed, Hillary dictated the following combat report:

> I took off with the squadron, the aircraft suffering from a damaged hood. Out over the sea east of Margate, we sighted 30 plus Me109s, 1,000 feet above us and coming straight. They came down and we split up. I climbed up and from slightly below and to starboard, opened fire with a three second burst on a 109 at 300 yards closing to 150. Bits came off but he did not go down. I continued firing in astern, burst of four seconds, closing in as I did so. He took no evasive action, burst into flames and spun towards the sea. I was hit from astern by incendiary bullet. The cockpit caught fire – I could not open the hood and passed out from the heat. When I came too I was free of the aircraft and pulled my 'chute and came down in the sea. Wing Commander Denholm will confirm destruction of enemy aircraft.

Hillary, as he was to admit in his book, had made the most commonly made error a fighter pilot can make, of following his enemy down and flying for far too long in a straight line. In his excitement he also forgot the golden rule of keeping a strict look-out behind and the price he paid was terrible. If it had not been for the damaged hood he might have got out and floated down to safety but the hood stuck leaving him inside the blazing cockpit. Once a fighter's cockpit was set on fire, it was estimated that the pilot had about seven seconds to get out before it became a raging inferno, with the heat rising to the equivalent of several well-functioning cooking ovens! Fortunately the Spitfire broke up but not before it had spun down from 25,000 to 10,000 feet. He was sent into space, where he regained enough of his senses to pull the ripcord of his parachute.

He splashed down into the sea fifteen miles east of Margate and spent three hours in the water while the Margate lifeboat searched for him. Feeling certain that he was doomed to die and realising too that he was badly burned, he decided to end it, releasing the air from his Mae West but his parachute lines which entangled him kept his head and face above the water. Then they found him. .

Number 603 Squadron had also lost Pilot Officer D. Stewart-

Clark, shot down by 109s, but although wounded he successfully baled out. They also shot down some 109s, one falling to Richard's friend Peter Pease, who sent his victim into the sea twenty miles north-east of Margate.

Hillary, however, had flown his last operational sortie. His book does tend to give an impression that he was in action for longer than he actually was, but in fact the short period is only emphasised when looking at his achievements as a fighter pilot. From the day he claimed his first victory, 29 August, till he went into the sea on 3 September, he had claimed five Messerschmitt 109s destroyed, two probably destroyed and another damaged. One can but only wonder what he might have achieved if he had survived longer.

*

From the time of his rescue, there began the terrible and agonising period of hospitalization. When his mother and father first saw him in hospital, they found him with his legs and arms heavily bandaged and held away from the bed by straps. His face was completely hidden beneath a mask of tannic acid (the current treatment for major burns) over which was a covering of gauze which hid from his parents the repellent sight of the mask. The room was in darkness and Richard was going through bouts of unconsciousness but was often quite lucid.

He spent three months in the Royal Masonic Hospital in London, and then went to a special hospital at East Grinstead. There followed months of operations, plastic surgery, skin grafts etc, under the skilled hands of Doctor Archibald McIndoe; Richard was just one of this great man's group of badly injured servicemen – his 'Guinea Pigs' as they were called. All the time, and especially later when he visited America where he wrote his now famous book, Hillary felt that because he had been knocked out of the war so early when so many of his friends and colleagues had been killed, that in some way he was inadequate, that he had not done enough, not done his share. His friend Peter Pease had died in action during the big air battle that raged on 15 September 1940. By some strange dreamlike state when Hillary was under the anaesthetic he had even seen him die, had seen him destroy a Messerschmitt, as indeed he did, and then himself be shot down.

Richard Hillary was eventually allowed to fly again, for his injured hands had not lost the touch with the controls of a Spitfire, although they were weak. He attended the RAF Staff College, and then was passed fit for flying duties by a medical board. He went to Charterhall in Berwickshire, but found himself flying twin-engined Blenheims. It was difficult for him as it took more strength to fly this light bomber; it would have been far better for him to have remained on single-seaters, but he tried, hoping to eventually go onto the Bristol Beaufighter.

Far more shattering for this sensitive young man was to find that the spirit of 1940 had passed. The comradeship that had existed within 603 Squadron during the Battle of Britain was gone. He was with a new and different generation of flyers.

Then on the evening of 8 January 1943 the aeroplane in which he was flying crashed and he was killed along with his navigator, Walter Fison. The flames which had reached for him in 1940 finally consumed him – and Richard Hillary, the epitome of the 1940 fighter pilots was no more.

8

Michael

The often used descriptive phrase, 'He was a typical fighter pilot ...', might or perhaps should, conjur up the picture of a tall, slim, good-looking chap with the shadow of a smile hovering at the corners of his mouth, and probably from a well-to-do or certainly upper middle class family. With a cheerful wave he would climb in the cockpit of his fighter plane, with a silk scarf at his throat, to roar into the heavens to do battle with the dreaded enemy.

Not all were like that, but some were. Many were very different. But for me, Michael Robinson falls into the category of a typical fighter pilot.

Certainly he was extremely good-looking, debonair, the son of Sir Roy (later Lord) Robinson, was always immaculately dressed, gave the impression of being a playboy (which was often misleading) and had that air of self assurance that was impressive. He had joined the Royal Air Force in 1935, training at No 3 FTS at Grantham, then in August 1938 had joined 111 Squadron, later being part of the unit's aerobatic display team. During his leave periods before the war he would fly around Europe in a small private aeroplane. He spent one week at a French air base on one occasion, flying their aircraft. On another visit he stayed at a German base but was not allowed access to their machines!

At the beginning of 1940 he was posted to France to join 87 Squadron but a crash just thirty-six hours before the Germans began their *Blitzkrieg* robbed him of the chance of meeting the enemy in the air during that campaign. Returning to England, which was something of an adventure in itself, he recovered from his hand injury by the summer, and as a flight commander with no combat experience, was sent to 601 Squadron, an Auxiliary Air Force unit famous for its well-off, playboy types. He was posted in on 18 August, the day Peter Walley died, and had his first successful action on the 31st.

At approximately 1 pm, 601 Squadron was scrambled to intercept bandits over Colchester at 15,000 feet. Thirty Dornier 17s escorted by Me109s above came into view. As Robinson approached the bombers from astern and to one side, he saw a 109 below, to his left. He dived at it but the 109 pulled up and the two fighters flew at each other head-on. The German pilot broke first; Robinson got on its tail, firing, which started the 109 smoking from the underside of the 109's engine cowling. He gave it another burst and it rolled over and dived inverted to the ground. A second 109 flew by. Robinson attacked this, giving it a short burst from the quarter. This too began to trail smoke, then dived vertically. Yet another 109 dived past him but Robinson was now out of ammunition. Nevertheless he chased after the 109 as it flew southwards at ground level.

The two fighters raced along, never rising above 100 feet, but well south of Maidstone the German pilot throttled back, allowing Robinson to formate on him. He indicated to the German that he must land, by pointing downwards but the 109 pilot turned away. Robinson then carried out a dummy quarter attack, breaking away very close to the 109. After that the enemy pilot landed in a field at about 140 mph, twenty-five miles south-east of Maidstone. Robinson circled watching as the pilot climbed out apparently unharmed holding his hands above his head. In his official report of this action, Robinson then said he waved, the German waving back, whereupon the British pilot flew over him and threw out a packet of 20 Players cigarettes. It was quite a unique victory especially a first victory and Robinson wrote in his flying log-book:

Intercepted 50 [sic] Do17s with Me109 escort over Colchester. Attacked and damaged two Me109s, ran out of ammunition and chased another thirty miles at ground level and persuaded him to land. Pilot appeared unhurt, threw him 20 Players.

This story became very well known at the time but what Michael Robinson did not admit to higher authority is that he landed in a nearby field and walked over to his victim. He found the German lying in the sun (it was a brilliantly warm day) and as Robinson approached, the German put his hand in his pocket. Robinson thought he was about to pull a gun out but the German only took out a comb to comb his hair. In perfect English the German asked why he hadn't fired at him. Robinson admitted he was out of ammunition and took him over to his Hurricane to prove it. The German's reaction is not recorded!

*

On 4 September, in the early afternoon, Robinson claimed the probable destruction of an Me110 with his Number Three. They had intercepted 50 Dorniers and 110s near Worthing, the 110s forming a defensive circle. One was trailing smoke from both engines and Robinson fired, sending the 110 onto its back, heading towards the sea. He emptied his guns in a head-on attack against another 110 but was unable to follow it down, for another 110 got on his tail, though the 110 did start smoking from its port motor.

Two days later Robinson led Yellow Section off with the squadron at 8.52 am, to intercept raiders above Mayfield at 15,000 feet, thirty-eight minutes later. High above he could see white condensation trails and the occasional glint of the sun on Me109s. One 109 dived down, going fast. Robinson dived after it and, as it pulled up and its pilot put his fighter into a half roll, Robinson opened fire as he too put his Hurricane into a half roll. The Messerschmitt started to smoke and continued down, Robinson keeping on its tail, snapping off quick bursts. Suddenly the 109's cockpit canopy blew-off and the aircraft rolled majestically onto its back. Robinson fired again and the tailplane, rudder and fin ripped away, sending the 109 into a left hand spin to crash.

Michael L. Robinson (not Lister-Robinson as so often quoted) did not score again until 25 September. Leading Red Section, he and Blue Section were scrambled to patrol base at 4.17 pm at 15,000 feet. Five minutes later he was ordered to the Plymouth area as a raid was coming in from the south-east. Arriving above the harbour town just after 4.30 they saw thirty Dorniers and twin-engined Me110s flying on a northerly course. Robinson continued flying west in order to get up-sun of the Germans. However, they went into a turn a few miles north of Plymouth, coming straight towards the Hurricanes. Both of 601's sections made attacks from a three-quarter front position in echelon port formation.

Robinson opened up on a Dornier, swinging round to come at it head-on but he did not see if he had hurt it as he flashed beneath it.

Michael Robinson

Biggin Hill, 1941. l to r: Flt Lt John Bisdee, Squdn Ldr Paul Richey, Gp Capt Dickie Barwell, Michael Robinson, and his father, Lord Robinson.

Pulling up under the Dornier formation on its south side, he saw five Me110s. Attacking one from dead astern from 150 yards, he let go the remainder of his ammunition into it. Both engines of the 110 began to smoke but he did not see it crash. He was credited with a probable. The Dorniers were in fact Me110Ds of EG (*Erprobungsgruppe*) 210, the escorting 110s from ZG (*Zerstorergeschwader*) 26. One 110 from the latter unit was shot down that day plus two others damaged.

It was very common in the height of battle during 1940 for Dornier 17s to be confused with Messerschmitt 110s. Each having twin engines and twin rudders pilots often reported action against the wrong type.

*

Robinson now left 601 Squadron, going to Middle Wallop to join 238 Squadron as a flight commander. He arrived on the 28th, arriving with another successful fighter pilot, Pilot Officer R.F.T. Doe, who already had an impressive personal score of victories. He came from 234 Squadron, having flown with P.C. Hughes.

Robinson was to have only one combat with 238 Squadron, but it was a great one. His only comment in his log-book, however, was:

Patrol over Swanage, intercepted 50 Me110s and Do215s over Portland. Led Squadron and carried out head-on attack, destroying two 110s and one 109, Landed at Exeter, no petrol.

Flying Hurricane R4099 (VK-S) he led nine Hurricanes away from Wallop at 4 pm and kept just below 10/10ths cloud at 4,000 feet for some time before flying through it on a gyro compass course. As he flew above Worth Maltravers at 15,000 feet, control informed him of enemy aircraft flying in from the south-east, and he led his Hurricanes to the west to get into the sun. Then they saw them, 3,000 feet below and about three miles away, south of Portland. With the sun behind them and in echelon port formation the three sections dived head-on at the Germans.

Robinson hurtled straight through the vic of enemy aircraft firing as he went, although much too fast to see what his firing had achieved. He then went at a straggling 110 giving it a three second burst from 300 yards. Oil spewed back over Robinson's cockpit windscreen. The 110 went over onto its back, shedding pieces, and following it down through cloud he saw it dive into the water about ten to fifteen miles south of Portland Bill.

Regaining height and trying to clear his oily windscreen, he then saw another 110 heading south at 7,000 feet. He closed in behind the German aeroplane, right in to 100 yards, then fired three one-second bursts which knocked pieces off its port engine – then it blew up. The 110 turned over and went into the sea still upside down about five miles south of his first kill.

He then flew north, crossing the coast at Portland, climbing above the cloud layer, seeing a large number of aircraft milling about at 25,000 feet right above what he thought was five Spitfires. These five were flying in line astern. Robinson climbed up at full throttle and in fine pitch, coming up beneath them. They were flying in a large circle towards the north. As he reached a height just 2,000 feet below them, he recognised them as Me109s! As he watched they all dipped a wing to look down at the lone Hurricane but continued circling, making no effort to come down. So Robinson went up!

It never ceases to amaze me that so often in reading combat reports, RAF fighter pilots seem quite calmly to take on these and even greater odds without, apparently, the slightest hesitation. Five to one, from underneath, without any element of surprise, and with still more enemy machines higher up. It seems foolish, yet this is what made our air fighters better than the opposition – provided they lived!

Robinson climbed inside the circling 109s, attacking the last one, firing a long burst of approximately six seconds from 300 to 200 yards. The 109 turned over onto its back and went down with black smoke coming from its engine and white glycol streaming from underneath. Bits also flew off the top of the Messerschmitt. He was unable to follow it down as the other 109s were still above, but they were obviously low on fuel for they all began to dive away to the south. He too was low on fuel but switching to his gravity tank was able to get down at Exeter to refuel. He had been up for nearly 2½ hours and had fired 2,700 rounds. 238 Squadron claimed a total of four destroyed plus two damaged for no loss. Bob Doe got a Heinkel.

On 4 October, Mike Robinson was given command of 609

Squadron, leaving 238 the next day, which if nothing else was a switch of aeroplanes, from the Hawker Hurricane to the Supermarine Spitfire. Yet in his first action in his new job it made no difference to his performance as a fighter pilot.

One interesting comment in 238 Squadron's War Diary was mention of Pilot Officer Doe receiving the DFC on 5 October. The diarist, Flying Officer A. David the adjutant, commented: '... he (Doe) has downed twelve sky rats!'[1]

*

At 3.24 pm on 7 October, 609 Squadron was scrambled to patrol base, then sent to Portland in company with Michael's former squadron, 238, who were flying to 609's left. Gaining 19,000 feet of height they saw enemy aircraft about fifteen miles off to the south. 238 Squadron suddenly appeared to break up and turn eastwards and at the same instant Robinson saw several Me109s above in the sun. It was extremely bright and as they were heading into the sun it became very difficult to pick out the fighters ahead of them. In addition they '... were rather embarrassed by the 109s still above us.'

Robinson (in L1096 PR-L) switched on his R/T, ordering the squadron into line astern then led them under the 109s and towards a circle of Me110s directly ahead. Following his first attack, Robinson climbed to attack a separate 110 from the rear. Coming in from one side, a Hurricane took a quick deflection shot at the German machine, but Robinson continued firing when the Hurricane broke away. The 110 dived vertically with its port engine smoking.

Finding himself clear of aeroplanes, he radioed 'Bandy' Control for the position of any hostiles, being informed of some over Lyme Regis at 15,000 feet. Flying to that position he saw another circle of Me110s ten miles north-west of Portland. He made an attack on one of them and it dived vertically into the ground about five miles north of the coast. These Messerschmitts were probably from ZG26 who lost seven of their aircraft during a raid on Yeovil.

---

[1] Later Wing Commander R.F.T. Doe DSO DFC and bar – he claimed 15 victories during the Battle of Britain.

Patrol base Angels 20. Two Me110s, one went in minus his tail south of Dorchester, the other about five miles out to sea.

His next comments in this log-book recorded mixed fortunes of his new squadron; the first for 15 October flying Spitfire R6979:

Patrol Winchester Angels 20. Ran into 109s and 110s above us in the sun. Broke up squadron.

Then on 28 November, again in R6979:

Squadron scramble. Squadron attacked by Me109s out of the sun and we claimed one Me109. John Dundas and Baillon shot down. [The 109's pilot was] Major Wick, CO of Richthofen Geschwader, [who had] claimed 57 victories.

This referred to the famous action when John Dundas shot down Helmut Wick, one of the Luftwaffe's top fighter aces, although he was then himself shot down by the German's wingman.

Michael Robinson received the award of the DFC during November. During the Battle of Britain he had destroyed six, possibly seven German aircraft, plus four others probably destroyed or damaged.

*

Having established himself as both a fighter pilot and successful squadron commander, he was still with 609 Squadron in the New Year of 1941, being part of Wing Commander 'Sailor' Malan's Biggin Hill fighter wing (together with 74 and 92 Squadrons). One of his flight commanders in 609 was Flight Lieutenant Paul Richey DFC who wrote the well-known book *Fighter Pilot*. Paul Richey was no stranger to Michael, far from it. They had gone to the same school, joined the RAF together and Richey had in fact married Michael's sister, thus becoming his brother-in-law.

As the RAF commenced its offensive actions against the Luftwaffe over Northern France, 609 Squadron and Michael Robinson were there. Flying a Spitfire II (P7881) on 7 May 1941, he damaged an Me109 over the Channel but the next day (it was his own birthday) he was able to write in his log-book:

Birthday party. Squadron's lucky day; attacked and destroyed six Me109s plus two probables without loss to ourselves. Shot down two weaving 109s and was attacked by a swarm near France.

It was late in the afternoon when 609 had been scrambled and ordered to patrol Maidstone at 15,000 feet. Robinson was then informed that there was a dinghy in the sea halfway across the Channel (with apparently an important German sitting in it). Given a course of 100°, they saw a rescue boat on fire off Dungeness with a pair of Me109s circling it. 609 was still at 15,000 feet but before they could attack the two 109s flew south. Coming down to 10,000 over Dungeness, two more 109s came near to the burning boat.

Ordering Yellow Section to remain over the boat at 10,000 feet as top cover, Robinson dived on one of the Messerschmitts and gave it a five second burst from 800 to 200 yards and sent it into the sea. Chasing the other 109 he finally caught it up five miles from the French coast, opened fire at 800 yards, closing right in to 100 yards, then 50. White and black smoke trailed back and the 109 landed on the water just off the coast.

At the moment of his second triumph, nine Me109s came at him from all directions. Robinson turned north at zero feet, his ammunition finished. A terrific dog-fight began as the other Spitfires and the 109s fought it out above the grey/green sea. Robinson constantly turned to face various 109s, his superb piloting skill making it impossible for the Germans to register even a single hit on his Spitfire. Four more 109s were claimed, Sergeant A.G. 'Goldy' Palmer shooting one off his Co's tail. A splendid painting by Frank Wooten of this action, hung for many years in Biggin Hill's officers mess and later in the mess at RAF Church Fenton.

*

As the summer progressed and the Biggin Hill Wing continued its operations over France, Michael Robinson was able to slowly add to his already impressive tally of German aircraft shot down. During June he damaged two Me109s and on 3 July, flying W3238 on a bomber escort mission over Hazebrouck on Circus No 30, he bagged a brace of Me109Fs.

Robinson was leading his squadron in loose fours. About five miles north of Hazebrouck he spotted a single 109F flying in a straight course which was converging with the Spitfires. Robinson half rolled and led Red Section down behind the German fighter. It was obvious that its pilot had not the faintest notion that he was in any danger for he took no evasive action whatsoever. Robinson got right in behind him, opening fire with both cannon and machine-guns at 50 yards. The 109 went down in small pieces.

That same afternoon, Circus 31, again against the marshalling yards at Hazebrouck, 609 was over St Omer when Robinson picked out nine or ten Me109s flying west about 3,000 feet above his squadron and about one mile ahead. At the same moment he saw two 109s, 3,000 feet below over Hazebrouck itself. As he led Red Section down, the second 109 dived rapidly away and the Number One went into a tight right-hand turn, Robinson had little difficulty turning inside it to fire a full deflection shot, but he missed. The 109 pilot used his 'HA-HA' extra boost (Fighter Command's name for when a 109 belched out exhaust fumes and sped away) and climbed quite suddenly. Robinson hammered at it from long range and started to follow as the 109 then went into a dive. Then, the 109 pilot, trying everything to get away, pulled up into a stall but Robinson was in a good position to give it all the rest of his ammunition, then had to break away rapidly to avoid a collision. As he turned and looked back he saw the 109 dive half inverted pouring out black smoke in a left-hand turn. Robinson followed it for about 6,000 feet, and then lost sight of it, but Sergeant J.A. Hughes-Rees saw its wings come off just before it hit the ground.

In his log-book Robinson noted his two victories, stating that one was a 'Stooge', the other 'not such a stooge'!

The next day near Bethune, he damaged a 109F, one of four he saw dive through the Spitfire escort. He fired at each as they passed through his gun-sight, one streaming smoke as hits registered. He damaged another 109F on the 8th while leading the wing on Circus 39, then with his fighting eye right in, scored four victories on 10, 11, 12 and 14 July.

As deputy wing leader he was now leading the wing quite often, as Sailor Malan was approaching the end of his tour as wing leader and was in need of a rest. On 10 July Robinson led 609 and the wing on Circus 42 to Hardelot. Sometimes it is difficult for the researcher to reconcile official combat reports with what a pilot may sometimes write in his log-book and the action on this date is a case in point.

In his combat report he stated that a 109F he attacked about thirty miles inland from Le Touquet went down at an estimated 450 mph IAS. As it increased its angle of dive '... both his wings parted company and from then on his rate of descent increased considerably'. In his log-book this fight is recorded for 24 July!

> Offensive Sweep. Me109 destroyed, Me109 damaged. Both wings came off at about 450; he went a little faster then!

Log-books can quite often be the more inaccurate due, in most instances, to the fact that pilots, especially busy squadron or wing commanders, quite often wrote-up their log-books several days after the events. Days, fights and air-battles often merged and became confused. The author found in his research on Wing Commander Ian Gleed DSO DFC (*Fighter Leader*, Wm Kimber & Co, 1978) that Gleed in fact had a junior officer fill in his log-book for him in 1942 and then he made his own comments at a later date, again, confusing one or two actions.

On 24 July, Robinson's combat report only claims a probable victory over a 109F, plus another damaged while over St Omer.

During Circus 44 on 11 July, at 2.45 pm when between Cassel and St Omer, Robinson saw Me109s climbing up through cumulus clouds about ten miles away, trying to gain height up sun from the Spitfires. Robinson, now a superb tactician as well as a brilliant air fighter, manoeuvred his pilots to a point of vantage above the 109s. Seeing ten 109s coming through cloud he kept formation, certain that more 109s were following. Sure enough another bunch came into view but he still did not attack. Then a third squadron of Messerschmitts appeared. Only then did he lead his pilots down behind the last group. Swooping down behind the last 109 he let go a long burst, raking the 109 from 700 to 150 yards. The German pilot pulled up into a left-hand turn, pouring out smoke, then he baled out. Group Captain Dickie Barwell DFC, Biggin's station commander flying in Robinson's section, got a second Me109, other pilots claiming two more. The wing leader had led the perfect 'bounce'.

The next day Robinson bagged another 109 south of Gris Nez at

1.40 pm. The whole action was a great victory for 609.

> Me109 destroyed (spun into town of St Omer). Squadron of 12 attacked 11, 7 destroyed, 4 probables – no loss to ourselves.

*

In that period of 1941 Michael was at the peak of his prowess as a fighter pilot. In addition to being deputy wing leader he was to continue all-out for his old 609 Squadron. Without doubt his whole life revolved about it and he commanded a great deal of respect from not only the pilots but also the ground personnel. He was often to be found in off duty moments, wining and dining at some of London's most exclusive restaurants or night spots but could also be completely in place in the most lowly pub or bar with his men. He would also go to great lengths to satisfy himself that the tactics used were correct and if anything came up in debriefing sessions, however slight, he would pursue the matter in order to be able to use it again in combat.

On 19 July during a sweep (flying W3184) he had a scrap with a 109 and damaged it but he'd been lucky:

> Offensive sweep, 109 damaged. I think this 109 was flown by an ace. He had many victory stripes on his rudder. Lucky he did not add any more!

Then came the fight on the 24th, 609 flying as top cover to the wing. The 109 he attacked went spinning down like a top but he did not see it crash.

*

In August Michael Robinson was awarded the DSO and took over command of the Biggin Hill Wing when Malan was taken off operations. By this time he had been officially credited with 16 combat victories, plus three more probables and at least eight damaged. He also received the Belgian Croix de Guerre. .

Leading the wing on 7 August on Circus 67, Robinson saw a Spitfire being bounced by a 109 and he pulled up right in front of the German fighter, making it swerve as the wing commander fired.

The 109 belched smoke and dived but he could only claim a probable.

During an escort mission on 19 August flying his personal Spitfire marked with his initials ML-R – a wing leader's prerogative, Flying Officer Vicki Ortmans, one of 609's Belgian pilots, went into the sea. The operation – Circus 81 – but also known as Operation Leg, was for a formation of Blenheims of 18 Squadron, one of which dropped a replacement 'tin-leg' for Wing Commander Douglas Bader DSO DFC who had lost one of his metal legs when he baled out of his crippled Spitfire earlier in the month. Robinson circled over Ortmans until the rescue launch was well on its way but ran short of fuel. However, he managed to struggle back to Manston where he crash landed.

Flying W3413 on 24 August he shot down a 109F off Dunkirk – the Messerschmitt crashing on the beach near Gravelines. His Number Two, Maurice Choron, a Frenchman in 609, shot down the German's wingman. Robinson's last victory came on the 27th, leading the wing to patrol Hazebrouck and St Omer. Four Me109s were circling Gravelines at 6,000 feet. He attacked them, sending one down inverted streaming black smoke. This brought Robinson's score to 18.

Rested from operations at the beginning of September his assessment as a fighter pilot, made by Dickie Barwell, was – 'Exceptional'. He was given command of RAF Manston until early October when he took a post as aide to the Inspector General of the RAF.

On 1 January 1942 Robinson took command of the Tangmere Fighter Wing which had once been led by Douglas Bader. He failed to return from a sweep on 10 April. At his death Michael Robinson had amassed more than 2,000 flying hours. His loss was mourned by many, not least by his old 609 Squadron.

9

Eric

In four editions of the *Aeroplane* magazine during September and October 1945, in celebration of the fifth Anniversary of the Battle of Britain, an article entitled 'One of the Few' was published. The article comprised the letters, in diary form, of a fighter pilot to his father during the period March 1940 to July 1941. Although the pilot's name was withheld at the time, identified only as a twenty-year old fighter pilot of 152 Squadron who received the DFC at the end of 1940, the pilot was in fact Eric Simcox Marrs. Eric Marrs, known as 'Boy' to his friends, came from Dover and was trained at RAF Cranwell.

The article and the diary give a tremendous insight into Boy Marrs' part in the battle and the *Aeroplane Monthly* magazine has generously given me permission to quote from it in telling this young man's story. Like reading the letters of Nigel Weir, we are privileged to have Eric Marrs' own words to recall and remember yet another of Britain's sons who, unhappily also made the ultimate sacrifice.

*

Following his basic training, Marrs progressed onto Hawker Hinds and then Gloster Gladiators. Like many of his contemporaries, once the war had started and he was busily preparing for it, he was eager for the Germans to start the action. Finally, on 17 March 1940, he was posted to 152 Squadron based at Acklington, arriving on the 25th. 152 Squadron was a Spitfire unit, commanded by Squadron Leader P.K. Devitt. On 26 March Marrs wrote: 'Life is quite interesting on the whole, but it ought to liven up soon if the Germans are going to do anything at all.' Then on 2 April, having progressed onto the squadron's precious Spitfires, Marrs recorded:

I have got on to Spitfires at last. I had my first trip on Sunday and it was rather hectic. They are very sensitive and delicate on the controls at low speeds and after the other aeroplanes I have been flying I found myself being very ham-handed with the controls. Apart from this, they are very nice machines. The view forwards and downwards is not too good but is otherwise excellent, though when coming in to land the approach is made with the nose up and that makes you very blind. A special curving approach is thus necessary, which only leaves you blind for the final hold off. The speed is not noticeable until you get near the ground. On the whole they are very gentlemanly aircraft and the only really bad habit is a tendency to tip up on to its nose very easily on the ground. This necessitates great care in using the brakes. There has been very little excitement here and we are all longing for the sight of a Hun.

By 21 April, before the balloon went up in France, but while the Germans were invading Norway, he wrote:

I am nearly up to operational standard on Spitfires having done about 10½ hours on them. Even when one is operational one gets plenty of training and practice flying, and as the Hun seems to be too preoccupied with Norway to do anything about Britain I expect to get a good deal more practice before I have to fly in earnest.

When the Germans invaded France and the Low Countries on 10 May, Marrs and his unit were still in the north, but continually on the alert. The squadron had its first warlike encounters while covering convoys in the North Sea. It also did some night flying, then in July came the move south. 152 was sent to Warmwell near the south coast in 10 Group and had its first major clashes with the Luftwaffe over the Channel in mid-month, but the main activity was further eastwards.

In a letter written on 19 July Marrs wrote:

Our squadron had another little engagement some days ago. They came up against some Ju87s escorted by Me109s and with a Do17 as a decoy. I say they because I was unfortunately at breakfast during this show and missed it. They shot down the

Do17, a Ju87 and the two Me109s confirmed, with one or two others rather doubtful. We had one pilot, Jumbo, shot down, but he got out all right with a leg wound and was picked up from the sea shortly afterwards. Since then things have been very quiet indeed round here. The Germans seem to be concentrating chiefly round Dover and Folkestone at the moment.

As August began, activity increased all along the south and on the 15th, Marrs had his first real combat, followed by his first success on the 16th. He wrote to his father the next day:

Well, I have been in the thick of things since I came back from leave. I found that we had had two casualties and that was the reason for my recall. One was a flight commander and the other was the chap who only got married about a month ago.

We had no shows that evening. Next morning we had to get up at 4.30, but had nothing to do till about 7 am. Three of us were then sent after some enemy aircraft floating round the countryside. One of them eventually popped out of a cloud not far from us. I managed to get within 500 or 600 yards, too far to fire, but he popped into another thick cloud. I went round the other side but lost him. The machine was a Dornier 17. The day then passed quite quietly though we flew quite a lot, until about 5.15 pm.

As many aircraft as possible were ordered into the air. Nine of us took off and climbed up to 15,000 feet over Portland. Soon we were told over the radio 'Many enemy aircraft approaching Portland from south.' About two minutes later I had my first sight of them. A cloud of black specks milling round and round, about half way across the Channel and about the same height as us. We climbed up another 2,000 or 3,000 feet up sun of them and about five miles south of Portland; and there they were. There must have been more than a hundred of them – Ju87s escorted by Me110s. The 87s were in Vees of three, in tight formation. They were more or less surrounded by 110s. Behind and to the right of and above these 87s was another formation of 110s.

I must say that at the sight of all these aircraft my heart sank. How could nine Spitfires stop all these? However, we were ordered into line astern and down we came out of the sun – straight in behind the bombers. That dive cheered me up no end. I was going too fast to get a good shot in (I shall know better next time), but sprayed an 87. Then down and to the left and up into the sun again. I looked for stragglers. There were German aircraft everywhere, though from after that first dive I never saw another Spitfire in the fight. I found a 110 fairly separated. I had a short dog-fight and managed to get several short bursts in but noticed no effects. Then away again. It isn't healthy to stay on one aeroplane for any length of time.

I looked for more stragglers and could find nothing that looked pleasant, so I just charged back into the main group of bombers. I was nearly head-on to them and opening fire at a fairly long range I plastered a Vee of three 87s but did not manage to put the *coup-de-grace* to any of them. I nipped under them at the last minute and went down in a dive. I then met up with another 110. I couldn't help it, there were so many of them. We circled around each other for a bit in tightening circles, each trying to get on the other's tail, but my attention was soon drawn by another 110. Down underneath him I went and pulled up giving him a long burst into the belly. Nothing seemed to happen.

I was then occupied by yet another 110. I milled around with him for a bit, but when I wanted to get in a shot I found I had run out of ammunition. I rolled on my back and pulled out of the mêlée and went home. I had unfortunately shot down nothing but as I came home I saw a Hurricane. Reinforcements had come up and were having their turn at the enemy.

Twenty minutes after that show three of us were up again, but it was all over.

Next morning we were up at 4.30 again. Nothing happened till lunchtime. We were sent up to 20,000 feet east of the Isle of Wight. When we arrived, enemy fighters materialised all around us. I was fully occupied with dodging and never had a chance to get my sights on anything. I finally went into a spin through doing too tight a turn at low speed. I came out and there was nothing in sight. I climbed up again towards the sun, and looked around. I saw about six aeroplanes bearing down on me from my left. I thought they were Spitfires and did nothing. When they were too close to be comfortable, they turned out to be Me109s. I did such a steep turn that I went into another spin. When I came out I had a good look round and then made for land. I must have been about twenty miles out to sea. I looked for trouble or friendly fighters and finally found five other Spitfires or another squadron. I stuck with them until I was short of petrol but saw nothing and finally had to return owing to shortage of petrol.

That evening we had another patrol. We saw nothing. Not long before we were ordered to land, I suddenly saw two Heinkel 111s stooging along below us. I called up the leader on the R/T and dived straight after them as they were going into a layer of thickish mist. I managed to keep sight of the rear one and when it came out the other side I was able to shoot it up. I left it with smoke coming from both engines and my own machine covered in oil from it. I don't think it could have got home and I'm pretty sure it didn't.

My R/T message was not understood and so nobody else saw them. I am counting that as my first. I returned home much cheered.

This last fight with the Heinkels occurred at 6.15 pm, ten miles south of Southampton at 3,000 feet. Marrs was flying as Blue 2. Calling Red 1, he then dived in order not to lose sight of them in the evening haze. He fired at 300 yards which produced goodly showers of oil which covered his windscreen, spinner and leading edges. Thinking the oil was coming from his own engine he broke away. When last seen the Heinkel's propellers seemed to be rotating slowly and smoke was coming from both motors.

Marrs received credit for one destroyed in his next action, on the afternoon of 18 August. 152, 43, 601 and 602 Squadrons got in amongst a large formation of Stukas off the Isle of Wight. These came from I and II Gruppes of Stukageschwader 77 (StG/77) and they lost 16 of their number to the Spitfires and Hurricanes. The Me109 escort from JG27 was engaged by 234 Squadron, in which one of the pilots was Flight Lieutenant Paterson Hughes.

Eric Marrs was flying as Black 2 when he found and dived on one group of thirty Stukas off Southampton. He singled out the second Stuka in line as they descended and headed for home. The dive-bombers began taking violent evasive action by flying in steep turns while flying fairly slowly, but Marrs got in a good deflection burst at 300 down to 50 yards and it caught fire at the port wingroot. As he broke off the action he saw the Stuka dive into the sea.

August 22. We have only had one show since I last wrote and that was the day after I wrote. It was the day the Germans lost about 150 aircraft. There was a large scale raid on Southampton and Gosport consiting of Ju87s escorted by Me109s. We arrived on the scene just as the 87s had finished dropping their bombs. There were other squadrons already there and we have since learnt that one of them took on the fighter escort. We were therefore lucky, and when we arrived we found about thirty Ju87s making for France. We dived after them and they went down to about 100 feet above the water. Then followed a running chase out to sea. The evasive action they took was to throttle back and do steep turns to right and left so that we would not be able to follow them and would overshoot. There were, however, so many of them that if one was shaken off the tail of one there was always another to sit on. I fired at about six and shot down one. It caught fire in the port wing petrol tank and then went into the sea about 300 yards further on. When I had finished my ammunition I turned away and found an Me109 sitting on my tail. As I turned it fired a burst in front of me. I could see the tracer and I seemed to fly straight through it. I was not hit, however, and ran for home as it was senseless staying without ammunition. I was not followed and two other chaps shot down that 109 soon after.

Yesterday our section found a Ju88 and shot it down and that now makes our squadron total of enemy aircraft confirmed to 33

On the evening of the day he wrote this account, he was in action north-west of Portland at 5.25 pm. He was now a section leader, leading Blue Section on this patrol, ordered to cover Portland at 16,000 feet. They were given a course to fly when his Number Three gave the 'Tally-ho' – aircraft seen and attacking.

It was a Dornier 17 which was making rapid progress towards the English coast. Marrs led his men down, overhauled the Dornier and got in a quick burst. Blue 2 became separated but Blue 3 attacked it and then broke away. Marrs came in again as the bomber headed for cloud. As his guns emptied they were down to 5,000 feet and he and his Number Three shared the German's destruction although it appears that the Dorner did in fact get back to France.

There followed a few days respite for 152 Squadron, but Boy Marrs wrote again on 27 August about the big fight which occurred on the 25th. Flying as Number Two to Black Leader, they had found the Germans five miles to the south-west of Portland about 5.35 pm at 8,000 feet. There were an estimated forty Ju88s, Me110s and 109s.

Our flight went into line astern to attack a formation of Ju88s but on the way in I, who was last of the string, became tangled up with some Hurricanes which I thought were Me109s. The bombers had disappeared by the time I had disengaged myself and I could not find anything to shoot at. Then I saw a lone twin-engined machine about five miles out to sea and about 5,000 feet below me making for France. I dived after it and found it was an Me110. When it saw that I was overtaking it, it whipped round and came head on at me. I held on as long as I could but he seemed to be going to ram me, so I pushed the stick forward hard and just went under his wing.

I went round in a steep turn and found he was doing the same in the opposite direction. I opened up my turn in order to give him a wider berth and then when I had passed him, steepened up again to come round on his tail. This I was able to do, and with a longish burst I put his port motor on fire. I then found myself overshooting. I throttled right back but could not pull up in time and drew out to his right. I overshot him by about 300 yards and I watched him over my shoulder. I saw him turning in behind me to get his sight on me and leaving it as late as possible so that he would not be able to follow me round, I went into a steep climbing turn to the left, going into it as quickly and violently as possible. His tracer passed under me. I continued my steep turn and came round behind him again. I took good care to stay where I was this time. With another long burst I put his starboard engine on fire and pieces flew off. I then left him. None too soon either, for I caught a glimpse of an Me109 diving down out of the sun on to what would have been my tail. I was now about twenty miles out to sea and I made for home at top speed. About half way back to land I passed six more Me110s going back to France. I did not stop to argue as I was still about ten miles out to sea. When I landed I found that I had a bullet through my oil tank and had lost nearly all my oil.

We lost two people that day and only had three confirmed and one unconfirmed. We were rather depressed that night. We have now lost six people since we have been here and the squadron score stands at 40 confirmed and 15 unconfirmed. I don't suppose we ought to complain really but it is always a blow when people don't return.

On the days following this action, the main battle swung to the south-east of England, and 10 Group's squadrons had something of a breather. In early September Marrs wrote about his Spitfire which he had named 'Old Faithful'. It was, he believed, the oldest on the squadron having accumulated about 300 flying hours. Marrs himself had flown 300 hours, 130 of them on Spitfires.

You were asking my score. It is $2\frac{1}{2}$ confirmed and 1 unconfirmed; the half being one I shared with another chap and the unconfirmed one being the Heinkel which I left with both engines giving off a lot of black smoke and which poured oil over my aeroplane. The two and a half consists of one Ju87, one Me110 and a half Dornier 17. I have shot down all these in my own aeroplane, which is another reason for calling it 'Old Faithful'.

*

The threat of invasion by the Germans was very prevalent as September began and following the enemy's first raid on London on the 7th, there was a good deal for Marrs to comment upon when he wrote to his father on the 10th:

How are things going with you with all this bombing of London? Poor old London! It has received a terrible hammering and so long as this moon lasts is bound to receive worse. The casualties are colossal. This is the sort of thing I have been expecting for a long time and it is what everybody thought would come at the beginning of the war.

We are still doing nothing down here. The Hun has been concentrating entirely on London just lately and it seems to go to show that Germany has not the colossal bomber force she claims to have, otherwise she would be able to concentrate on a greater number of places at the same time.

I am glad we did not waste time and bombs on large-scale reprisals against Berlin. If the invasion is going to come before next spring, I feel it must come during this moon and concentrations of shipping at Channel ports, etc, seem to show that they may be going to have a crack at it soon and that we should waste bombs on Berlin is probably just what Hitler would like.

Our squadron is now up to strength again and we have managed to train quite a number of new pilots during the lull in operations down this way.

The battle came into 10 Group's area on the 15th and 17th. Marrs got into the scrap on the 15th and was then involved above Shepton Mallet in Somerset on the 17th, chasing a lone Ju88 shortly after lunch. He was leading Blue Section patrolling Portland when he was ordered to fly a course of 350° and told to climb to 20,000 feet. After eight minutes came a change of course to 280°. Then he saw the bandit, a Junkers ahead and climbing with dark camouflage and a white band around the fuselage. Marrs radioed the 'Tally-ho', ordered his section into line astern and attacked.

We have had some more excitement during this last week [he wrote on the 22nd]. Last Sunday, the famous day of the 185[1], we had thirty He111 bombers over Portland. There was only one flight up at the time and I was leading it. A flight is six aircraft. I had been patrolling the aerodrome for some time already with one other chap, when the other four were sent off to join me. Before we had joined up we were sent off to intercept this raid

[1] At the time the RAF claimed the destruction of 185 German aeroplanes.

coming in from the SW of Portland Bill.

I was over Weymouth when I first saw them. They were coming at Portland from the west. I climbed up to come in behind them from the sun, but they were going faster than I thought. They were in tight formation and they dropped their bombs on Portland Bill from 16,000 feet, doing pattern bombing. We then came in on their tails and they turned out to sea. We chased them for about ten miles, nibbling at the rear end of their formation, and we knocked down two of them. I myself did not get one, though I must have damaged two of them. If we had had the whole squadron up we could have broken up their formation and knocked down quite a number. The extraordinary part about this raid was that there was no fighter escort.

On Tuesday I was leading a section of three and we were ordered onto a Ju88 bomber up near Bath. I attacked first and hit the radiator of his starboard engine with my first burst. His glycol poured out in white streams and his starboard motor finally packed up. The other two then attacked in order and then we each nibbled around attacking when we could. He then managed to reach the clouds which were thick puffy cumulus. I followed him into one and lost him. I circled round looking for him and then noticed a strange smell. I looked down and saw slight fumes arising from under the dashboard. During the scrap I had noticed an aerodrome with big runways standing out and showing up well. ...

Eric Marrs got down safely although the airfield was under construction and covered with concrete blocks to prevent German transport aircraft from landing there. He found one bullet had got through his oil cooler and his engine seized as he descended. Later, on returning to his base, news came that the Ju88 had come down at Imber, a small village three miles from Dauntsey not far from Swindon.

The next day he and two others drove to the crash. Two of the crew had been killed and one wounded; only the pilot was unhurt although the RAF pilots inspected four bullet marks in the armour plate behind the pilot's seat. However, his Spitfire, Old Faithful, had to go to an MU for major repair and due to its age, Marrs did not expect to fly it again. The Ju88 was from II/LG1 and it was

shared between Marrs, Sergeant K.C. Holland and Flying Officer
P.G. O'Brian. 152 Squadron and Boy Marrs were in action again on
the 25th, and Marrs damaged three German machines south of
Bristol at 11.30 am. It proved to be quite a scrap:

On Wednesday morning A flight was sent off to patrol. Soon
afterwards the rest of the squadron was told to get into the air as
quickly as possible. The result was we all went off in bits and
pieces. I went off with one other chap and as a pair we went
looking for trouble. We climbed up to 16,000 feet and saw a
tremendous cloud of aircraft just round Yeovil way going north.
There were two large groups of bombers consisting of about forty
bombers each. Milling around and above them were numerous
Me110s acting as guard.

Well, the two of us proceeded north, passed the enemy and
came round in front of them. We waited just south of Bristol for
them. Then we attacked. We went head-on straight for the
middle of the foremost group of bombers. Firing as we went we
cut through the heart of them like a knife through cheese; but
they wouldn't break. They were good, those Jerry bombers –
they stuck like glue.

On coming through the first group I ran into some Me110s. I
milled around with those for a bit trying to get on the tail of one
of them, but there was always another to get on my tail. Things
became a bit hot and seeing a 110 very close to getting a lovely
shot in on me, I pulled the stick back hard and pushed on full left
rudder. I did three smart flick rolls and spun. I came out of the
spin below everything. I climbed up to sunwards of everything to
have another crack at the bombers, climbed to the same height
and slightly in front of them on their starboard side. I saw a
Heinkel lagging behind the formation and dived to attack it from
the starboard quarter. I put a long burst into it and it also
streamed glycol from its starboard engine.

My attention was then occupied by an Me110 which came to
the help of the Heinkel. A steep turn was enough to get behind it
as it did not seem very anxious to stay and fight. I came in from
the starboard quarter again and kept my finger on the firing
button, turning in behind it. Its starboard engine (becoming a
habit now) streamed glycol.

Suddenly there was an almighty bang and I broke away quickly. I looked around, glanced at my engine and oil tanks and positioned myself for another attack, this time going for the port engine. I just began to fire when my ammunition petered out. I broke away and dived below cloud, throttled back, heaved a deep sigh and looked around to see where I was. I steered south, came to the aerodrome and landed. I had a look at my machine and counted eleven bullet holes in it. The one that made the bang in my cockpit had come along from the rear, nipped in the right hand side of the fuselage and smashed the socket into which the R/T is plugged.

Two days later, Boy Marrs scored another victory. It was 27 September.

Friday was a good day. I set the ball rolling by finding a lone Ju88 at 23,000 feet. I had a long running fight during which we came down to 50 feet and skimmed the hills of Devon. I did continuous quarter attacks aiming at his engines and was able to hit both of them. Glycol streamed forth and I hovered around waiting. As I expected both engines soon stopped. He made for the south coast of the Bristol Channel and landed about 20 yards from the beach in the water, running his machine up onto the beach. I circled round and watched the crew get out. They waved to me and I waved back, and then hordes of civilians came came rushing up. I watched the crew taken prisoner, beat up the beach and then climbed away. The place he came down was Porlock and no doubt you heard that little engagement mentioned over the wireless on the news that night. Well, his rear gunner had landed a few bullets in my machine. On had penetrated the leading edge of my machine, going through the well into which the wheel was retracted and puncturing the tyre. One other had landed in the fuselage about six inches from my left knee.

In the afternoon, 152 Squadron claimed four enemy aircraft without loss but Marrs, with his Spitfire damaged, missed the action.

*

As October began, 152 Squadron celebrated its 60th victory with a party in Swanage where most of the pilots got rather the worst for wear. Marrs was more than happy to celebrate for he had been lucky to escape another close call on the last day of September. He had been bounced while attacking some 110s. The whole world seemed to tumble in on him and petrol began to pour into the cockpit. A bullet knocked off the starter button on the dashboard before going out through the windscreen. The bullet which punctured the fuel tank had previously smashed away one of the petrol taps right in front of him, splinters from the bullet becoming embedded in his leg. Going home as quickly as possible, smoke began to appear from behind the instrument panel so he switched off his engine, glided towards the airfield, switching on the engine again as he came in. Only he found that just one wheel came down, the other remained persistently up. However, he got the machine down without serious damage, and was praised for the way in which he landed.

On 7 October, Marrs led Blue Section (in R6968) east of base in the afternoon, to attack fifty Ju88s, Me110s and Me109s. In the fight Marrs shot down a 110 which was painted white from the nose back to the cockpit.

> The bombers were in loose formation at about 16,000 feet with their guard of Me110s behind and above them. We were at 20,000 feet and to one side of the bombers. We all dived down on the latter to try and split them up thoroughly. I was not able to get in a good shot at them and pulled away to the right and up again. I then took stock of the position. I was in a bad position to go for the bombers again so I thought I would have a crack at the fighters. These I found were going about in strings of about ten aircraft sneaking along behind the bombers. From time to time the leader of each string would come round behind the last man in the string to form a defensive circle. The leader would then break the circle again to catch up the bombers.
>
> After one or two attempts I found I was able to sneak up behind one of these 'strings' and attach myself to the end of it for a short spell, shooting at the end machine in the line. Everytime the leader came round to form a defensive circle I had to break away and wait till the circle broke up again. In this way I was

able to make the end of one of these lines stream glycol from one of its engines. I was not able to finish it off as the leader of this particular string was forming one of the defensive circles and was coming round behind me.

The Huns were now making for the coast again and I saw a straggler all by himself. I swooped up on him from the starboard rear quarter. He saw me coming and opened up, but I was able to catch him up easily. I opened fire and his starboard engine streamed glycol. I switched on to the fuselage and then over to the port engine. I was by now overtaking him somewhat fast, so I drew out to his left. Suddenly the back half of his cockpit flew off and out jumped two men. Their parachutes streamed and opened and they began drifting slowly earthwards. Their aeroplane, left to itself, dived vertically into the sea, making a most wonderful sight and an enormous splash. I had not finished my ammunition and looked around for something else to shoot at, but everything seemed to have cleared off, so I circled round the two Huns, now floating earthwards. They took an awful long time to come down on land and I watched the army rush up to capture them.

The Messerschmitts came from II and III Gruppes of ZG26 during an attack against Yeovil. At least seven were shot down by 152, 238 and 601 Squadrons. It was not all one-sided, for 152 lost two machines (one pilot wounded), 238 lost one and 601 another damaged.

As the battle began to end, Marrs went on leave and upon his return to duty there was a lull in German activity over the west country. Occasionally 152 went up after high flying Me109s but it was another Ju88 which Marrs and his section shot down on 14 November, Boy flying R6968. They got the 88 west of Shaftesbury.

We continue to get an occasional fighter sweep over the Isle of Wight or that district, but have not connected up with any of them. I have had some luck, though, in that I met up with a lone Ju88 the other day. I was leading a section of two when we saw a condensation trail moving across above us about 5,000 feet higher. We turned round and climbed flat out after it. It was going north and it took us some time to catch up, so when we did it was well inland. I was able to get within about 800 yards of it before it saw me, and when finally it did see me it began a gentle turn to the left. This was very nice for me and I was able to close in and give it a burst from the port rear quarter. I made three attacks from port and starboard quarters but could see no visible result from my fire. I therefore thought to myself, 'Damn this', and coming in from dead astern and slightly underneath I held my fire until within about 150 yards. I then gave it a good burst at point blank range and smoke began to come from the port engine. Unfortunately the rear gunner of the 88 landed one plumb on the middle of my windscreen splintering it in all directions and making it quite opaque.

I drew away to the left and saw that I had started a fire under the port engine, an ominous red glow being clearly visible. I could not sight any more through my cracked windscreen but my Number Two was going hard at it. All this time the enemy had been diving hard south. We had caught him up at 24,000 feet and had now got down to about 5,000 feet and were over Poole. The Hun was now obviously in a bad condition and badly on fire. He began a left-hand turn which became steeper and ended in a vertical dive. He hit the ground over the vertical, on a street corner in Poole. There was a great mushroom of orange flame edged with oily black smoke, as all his bombs exploded with his petrol.

I dived down to have a look and could see nothing left of the aeroplane except a large number of little pieces scattered over a wide area, and each burning fiercely. There were also three houses on fire and I was very sorry about that. It was a pity it could not have come down in a field. Luckily there were no civilian deaths, though I believe two people were injured. I had six bullets in my machine. Two through the prop, one on the windscreen, one in the wing and two others had penetrated the engine cowling, one bouncing off the crankcase and the other half severing three plugleads and finishing up in the fireproof bulkhead.

His Number Two in this action was Sergeant A.W. Kearsey (P9427) who closed to 150 yards also, after his leader had completed three attacks. Kearsey saw the inside of the 88's fuselage on fire but continued his attack. He watched as the bomber lost height and crashed at Parkstone. Of the several bullets that hit Marrs' machine, by far the most striking to see was the one which hit dead centre of the windscreen. Those who saw it marvelled that the bullet did not penetrate and went to show how the windscreen could stand up to the hardest blows. This undoubtedly cheered the RAF pilots of 152 Squadron.

*

Boy Marrs' last victory of 1940 (again flying R6968) came on 28 November. A lunch-time sortie interrupted their meal, the pilots rushing into the air then flying towards the Isle of Wight. Above them flew several formations of Me109s and despite a hard climb by the Spitfires, the 109s remained high above them. Then, the 109s became aggressive and began to come down, the Spitfires turning to meet them. With surprise lost, the 109s started to climb back out to sea. 152 returned to base.

The pilots remained on the ground until tea-time. Marrs was just in the process of eating a piece of bread when the alarm sounded and they were off yet again. It was just after 4 o'clock.

Once more we were sent off late, and we were only at 23,000 feet over the Isle of Wight when we saw the blighters coming in above us at about 30,000 feet. We were not making condensation trails at 23,000 feet but the Huns were, and when we saw some of the trails stop we knew they were coming down on us.

The next thing that happened was that, on looking over my right shoulder, I saw one of those beastly yellow-nosed blighters about a hundred yards on my right. It had obviously dived down and had a pot at somebody in our formation and I must have first seen him just after he had finished shooting. My instinctive reaction was to pull up sharply to the right to see if anything was coming down on my tail. As I did this, the Me109 slid across under me to my left and dived full speed for France. I flipped over to the left and dived flat out after him. The 109 was very keen to get home, and was a fool or over-confident, for he never looked round once to see whether he was being pursued or not.

It took me time to catch up, especially as I was not such a fool and weaved slightly to keep a look out behind my tail. I was very angry with him for having surprised us and I knew that one of us must have been shot up by him. I distinctly remember muttering to myself as I flipped over and dived after him, "You dirty b.....! This is where you get yours!"

I crept up on him slowly, keeping beneath him in his blindest spot. Slowly he got bigger in my sights – then he was in range, but I did not open fire; I was going to make absolutely sure of him, so I waited till I was within about 100 yards. Then aiming carefully I fired – a one second burst was enough. Black smoke belched forth and oil spattered over my windscreen. He half-rolled and dived away. I followed in a steep spiral to see what was going to happen but my speed became so great I pulled away and my wing hid him for a bit.

When I looked again there was a large number of flaming fragments waffling down to the sea. One large black lump, which was not on fire, trailed a white plume which snapped open and became a parachute. This was the pilot and he must have baled out just before the petrol tank blew up. However, he landed in the sea and might just as well have blown up for he was never found.

I went home in great spirits but this joy soon evaporated, for when I landed I heard of the death of the chap who had been flying just behind me. The 109 had shot at him, hitting his glycol system. Streaming smoke, he made for land and then tried to bale out. He bungled up his baling out and tore his parachute in doing so, with the result that his descent to earth was somewhat swift. His parachute streamed out behind him but owing to the tears did not open. We lost one other pilot that day, one of the Polish sergeants. He just disappeared and must have become involved with a large number of enemy fighters. So we lost two for two and that is not very satisfactory.

I found that I had shot down my 109 with 440 rounds, that is 55 rounds from each gun. This is the easiest victory I've had and fulfilled a long-felt ambition to shoot down one of those damned yellow-nosed blighters.

My total score is now six and a third confirmed, one unconfirmed and four damaged and is made up as follows: Destroyed confirmed: A half Dornier 17, one Ju87, one and a half [Ju88] and [a one-third] Ju88, one Me109, two Me110s.

Probably destroyed: One He111. Damaged: Two He111s, two
Me110s.

The Messerschmitt pilot shot down by Marrs, had hit Pilot Officer
A.R. Watson (R6597), Marrs' Number Two, who was also a
particular friend of his. Several pilots saw Watson try to get out and
Pilot Officer C.S. Cox saw him fall and his parachute fail to open.
Watson and his wrecked Spitfire were later found just south-east of
Wareham.

The Polish pilot was Sergeant Z. Klein. Pilot Officer F.H.
Holmes caught sight of a Spitfire and what appeared to be a flash,
then it spun away. This was the same action in which 609
Squadron was involved, or at least in the same locality. In their
fight they lost John Dundas, the Germans lost Helmut Wick, one of
their top pilots.

Shortly after this action, Eric 'Boy' Marrs was awarded the DFC,
which was Gazetted on the last day of the momentous year of 1940.

*

Early in the new year he shot down a Dornier 17Z north of
Warmwell, at 2 o'clock on 4 January. In R6968, he led Green
Section off on a scramble an hour earlier but after a search during
which he became separated from his Number Two, he returned to
base to ask for further information. Breaking below cloud at 4,000
feet he was told that the raider was now flying north towards
Warmwell at 5,000 feet. The next day he wrote:

I nipped up through the clouds quickly and circled around to
look. I had made one complete turn when I saw an aeroplane
about three miles NE of me, about 2,000 feet higher up, and
going WNW. I opened up everything and aimed to cut it off. It
looked very slim and had two rudders, and I thought it might
have been a Hampden, although I was pretty sure it was a
Dornier. I soon came close enough to see a large black cross on
its side and recognised it as a Dornier 17.

I approached from the sea and opened fire at about 400 yards
from the port rear quarter. He then turned south and dived like
stink for the clouds. I turned in behind him and, closing to about
250 yards, fired at the fuselage and two engines in turn. Black

and white smoke came from the engines and all return fire from the gunners ceased. I was overshooting and just before he reached the clouds I had to break away. I shot on down through the clouds and came out just over Weymouth Bay. I then hunted up and down above the cloud and below but not another sign of the Dornier did I see. I was very disconsolate and was sure he must have got away so I returned home and landed. I was therefore overjoyed to hear that he had come down in the sea and that boats had gone out to look for survivors. He had evidently turned left in the cloud and come out over Lulworth Cove. He appeared to be in difficulties and had smoke coming from him. He dived down to sea level going towards Portland Bill and then tried to climb up again. He was not able to and he came down in the sea about five miles SE of Portland Bill. A couple of waves washed over him and he sank. Nobody was found. Needless to say there was rejoicing in Bournemouth last night. I must say I have been phenomenally lucky with these lone aircraft and this was the first Hun that anybody had seen close enough to engage since those Me109s we were attacked by.

On March 28th he wrote:

Here I am back at Warmwell again after a very full day at Southampton and a number of shocks this morning. I was told when I got back this morning that my best friend, Charles Davis,[1] had been killed in a crash two days ago. It appears he flew into a hill when coming down through cloud near Winchester. His death has shaken me a lot.

I was told that I have been mentioned in despatches although what for I can't think.

The last thing I found out was that Dudley Williams[2] and I have to go to Buckingham Palace on Tuesday. We have to be there not later than 10.30 am and will receive instructions there.

The last shock was to find in a new casualty list, just out, that two more of my term at Cranwell, both of whom I know quite

[1] Flying Officer C.T. Davis DFC, 238 Squadron, scored several victories in 1940.

[2] Pilot Officer W.D. Williams DFC of 152, survived the war.

well, are now dead ... All this news being sprung upon me within about half an hour just about stopped my brain from working at all.

*

In April 152 Squadron moved to Portreath where it patrolled and flew convoy patrols. They also returned to night flying duties. Boy Marrs became a flight commander, after a short spell as an acting commander, and of this he wrote:

> It does not look as though any flight lieutenants are going to be posted to the squadron, and now I am well settled into my job. Whether I am doing it efficiently or not I don't know – I have had damn little experience of dealing with and handling men, but I am learning.

During the first half of 1941 it was pretty quiet for 152 down in Cornwall and it was not until July that Marrs had his next encounter. It was on the 18th. That afternoon, in P8237, he led Blue Section out over the sea towards the Isles of Scilly, being vectored towards a bandit. They found it, a He111, just above a layer of cloud and into which it flew. As they circled to the south-west of the islands in clearer sky, their patience was rewarded when the Heinkel appeared beneath the clouds. Marrs and his wingman, Sergeant E.H. Marsh (P8446) attacked and the German's starboard engine streamed glycol and oil smoke. The Heinkel went down to sea level, jettisoned its bombs and began to leave an oily trail on the water. The two RAF pilots continued to attack, their bullets kicking up the water all round the enemy machine. It finally made a right hand turn, hit the sea and blew up.

The following day he wrote to his father:

> ... Talking of shooting – I, with my number two, was lucky enough to come across a lone Heinkel 111 – one of these sea raiders – about twenty miles south-west of the Scilly Isles. We fixed it good and proper, and shot its tail off. It made a lovely splash in the sea – nobody got out ...

The squadron began flying escort missions from Portreath, to RAF bombers raiding the enemy naval base at Brest. On the afternoon of

24 July, 152 Squadron provided close escort to Hampden bombers against Brest, the raid being recorded as the biggest daylight attack of the war thus far. The RAF completed a successful raid but 152 Squadron lost two of its pilots. Sergeant Short was one, Flight Lieutenant E.S. Marrs DFC (in P7881) was the other.

Flak over the target was terrific and it was believed by the other pilots that it shot down both Short and Marrs. Short was thought to have been taken prisoner but Boy Marrs, who had celebrated his twentieth birthday just fifteen days before, was killed. 152 Squadron's diary recorded:

> He had been the B Flight Commander for a long time and was probably the best pilot in the squadron. Apart from that his personality and ability as a flight commander were supreme. He was admired and loved by everyone. His name in the squadron will live for evermore.

In the best traditions of the Royal Air Force, his fellow pilots had a tremendous thrash in the mess that night to send off their lost friend and comrade. When the party ended, everything that would break was suitably disposed of, most of it being thrown over the staircase into the hall below. When the CO returned in the early hours (and having seen gun flashes in the sky) and entered the mess he thought the building had been bombed. Fortunately a local benefactor came to 152's financial rescue and paid for the damage resulting from Boy Marrs' farewell party.

10

Paterson

It is true to say that there are several kinds of fighter pilot. Whatever war they have, or will be engaged in, their fortunes vary considerably. Each is possessed of his own individual skills which hopefully he would get to use to advantage, but that often used word 'luck' so often plays a vital role in a man's fighting career.

When studying the exploits of World War One fighter pilots, or scout pilots to use the correct term for that conflict of 1914-18, it soon became apparent to me that, broadly speaking, the successful 'aces' (for the want of a better term) quite often fell into two distinct categories. Firstly, there were those men who doggedly remained in action for long periods during which time they gradually amassed a respectable score of enemy aircraft brought down. Sometimes these pilots survived the war, some of them did not. Their luck, if you like, finally ran out – or they were simply caught out by a better pilot, or by a better shot.

The second category was the pilot who seemed to quite suddenly burst onto the scene and in a sometimes quite astonishingly short period of time, weeks, sometimes even just days, these men would produce a phenomenal rate of scoring. All too often these pilots would themselves be killed, wounded or captured fairly quickly, seeming to burn themselves out like some brilliant fiery meteor. If they were not killed they would end this short run of spectacular achievement, this exceptional moment and either not see further combat or just not score again.

This happened in the Second World War too; some pilots, some whose names became famous and well known to the general public, flew actively on and off for long periods before either being lost in action or just simply pulled out of the fighting, their job done. Several of the high scoring German pilots just had to remain in the front line due to an eventual shortage of experienced men and thereby these pilots amassed some very high combat scores.

All this was no less true during the Battle of Britain, some pilots surviving to go on to further feats of prowess over Europe or in the Middle or Far East. Others like those fiery meteors of the First War, just seemed to shine brilliantly for just a short time, then fade and die. Their luck suddenly deserted them. One of these was Flight Lieutenant P.C. Hughes of 234 Squadron.

*

Paterson Clarence Hughes was an Australian from Haberfield, New South Wales. He was born in the town of Cooma, New South Wales on 19 September 1917. Coming to England he became a regular RAF officer in Britain's peacetime but rapidly expanding Air Force, and following a successful training period, served in 64 and 247 Squadrons.

Soon after the outbreak of WW2, in November 1939, he was posted to 234 Squadron as B Flight Commander. During that first winter and into the spring of 1940 he helped to train the newly arrived pilots and forge the squadron into as an efficient fighting unit as its leaders could produce, to be ready for the conflict that all knew would soon come. By July 1940 they were as ready as most of Britain's other fighter squadrons – only the test of real action would prove how efficient they had become. If then, the pilots could learn quickly and survive their first taste of action they might manage to be a useful part of Britain's air defences.

Number 234 Squadron, code-named 'Cressy' in 1940, was equipped with Spitfires and based at Church Fenton until June, having been operational for just one month. The 1 it was sent to St Eval in Cornwall. Its first CO was Squadron Leader W.A.J. Satchell. The new squadron's chance to score its first victory came early in July when the Germans began testing Britain's defences in the opening phase of the Battle of Britain. On 8 July, shortly before tea-time, Blue Section, led by Flight Lieutenant Hughes, was 'scrambled' to provide protection for a convoy. Leading two other pilots, Pilot Officer K.A. Lawrence and Sergeant G.T. Bailey, Hughes found and intercepted a Junkers Ju88 flying just above a layer of cloud at 2,000 feet, twenty-five miles south-east of Land's End. Pilot Officer Lawrence attacked first and as he broke away, Hughes came in from astern, opening fire with only slight deflection. The Junkers climbed steeply into a higher layer of cloud,

Hughes following, and continued to fire at the greyish shape of the enemy machine at ranges between 30 and 50 yards, the rear-gunner returning fire. Then suddenly they both emerged from the white opaque cloud. The Australian fired twice more as the 88 went into a shallow dive and then broke away and downwards, its rear-gunner still firing. Hughes had fired a total of 2,494 rounds, and his Spitfire (P9366) had received one bullet through its leading edge of the starboard wing. 234 Squadron and Paterson Hughes, had opened the account against the Luftwaffe.

P.C. Hughes had got in close, never further away than 150 yards, sometimes as close as 30 yards. As the battle and the war progressed it became a fact that the closer a pilot could get to the target the more certain he was of making a kill. Quite often some of the best pilots were notoriously poor exponents of aerial gunnery. Those who appreciated this deficiency soon found that by using their flying skill to get in really close, their poor shooting ability was not too much of a handicap. When in close and being able to stick with a twisting, turning opponent, they invariably just couldn't miss. Hughes was always in close. It gained for him many successes but was eventually to be the cause of his downfall.

*

Hughes and his Blue Section found another Ju88 in precisely the same position off Land's End on 27 July, shortly after 3 pm. In company with Flying Officer F.H.P. Conner and Sergeant Bailey, Hughes had been ordered to patrol off the Cornish coast at 10,000 feet but were then instructed to climb to 23,000 feet when Radar picked up a 'bogey'. Hauling his Spitfire (N3280) up to that height and heading south-eastwards, they spotted the Junkers above but the German pilot seeing the three British fighters, inexplicably left the more safe altitude and dived vertically, probably hoping his speed would keep him safe from harm. He was wrong.

Hughes was after it, closing to 200 yards in a screaming dive, seeing clearly its brown and green camouflage patterns. Its rear-gunner began to fire back at the Spitfire as Hughes opened fire with a two-second burst from dead astern. Tracer bullets zipped back at him from both the 88's top and ventral gun positions, and as in his previous encounter, his machine was hit by a single bullet in its mainplane.

The 88 was now diving at an estimated speed of 300 mph and Hughes' next burst shattered the perspex of the top cockpit area, the top gunner's fire ceasing abruptly. Bits also flew off both of its engines and soon after his guns emptied, the 88 was still diving steeply. Initially the 88's destruction was unconfirmed but later it was known to have gone into the sea, twenty-five miles off Land's End. The German machine was from I/KG51, flown by Leutnant Ruckdeschel.

Early the following morning, the 28th, B Flight was at dawn readiness and at the ungodly hour of 4.25 am, Blue Section were scrambled to investigate a presumed bandit over Plymouth. As Hughes and his two wingmen, Pilot Officers K.S. Dewhurst and P.W. Horton arrived over the harbour town they saw bursting AA shells in the morning sky, then spotted yet another Ju88. It was diving steeply towards what seemed to be some object on the land. Hughes went down with it but waited until the Junkers began to pull up before he attacked. He opened fire at 100 yards, closing to 50, then held this position, snapping off short bursts as the enemy machine began a slight turn. Oil and greyish-yellow smoke began to trail back from the 88's starboard engine and then what appeared to be a red-hot object broke away from it. The 88 continued to fly on at a now low altitude while Dewhurst and Horton each made separate attacks upon the German. The bomber finally climbed slightly, then the starboard engine burst into flames and the machine slowly turned to starboard and hit the water. It sank below the waves in just ten seconds, none of its crew being seen to emerge before it did so.

The German rear-gunner had fired back at the Spitfires throughout the engagement and yet again Hughes' machine (N3239) had been hit by a single bullet, this one gouging a hole in the radiator fairing. Like the previous Ju88, this one too had been camouflaged green and brown and the forefront of its nose section was painted red. The machine came from II/LG1, and was flown by Leutnant Pfanf.

*

Three Ju88s claimed as destroyed in three weeks set Hughes on the road to stardom but it was to be the next phase of the battle which made him really famous although he was destined not to survive it.

Paterson Hughes

Hughes, second from left with pilots of 234 Squadron outside the scramble hut.

As the second phase opened at the start of August, 234 Squadron were more than ready for the fight. It was also about to get a new commanding officer when Satchell left to command 302 Polish Squadron. His place was taken by Squadron Leader J.S. O'Brien, who had been attached to 92 Squadron. He joined 234 Squadron on 17 August, as the squadron moved to Middle Wallop.

Thus it was that Hughes led 'Cressy' Squadron on the evening of 16 August. He headed eleven Spitfires on patrol at 16,000 feet near the Isle of Wight. At 6.15 pm he picked out a large gaggle of fifty Messerschmitt 109s flying 4,000 feet above them. Hughes led the squadron in line astern, climbing to 22,000 feet as the 109s formed a circle. Making his first attacking pass, Hughes fired a deflection shot at the 109 nearest to him which had just pulled round to attack Blue 3. Following a quick burst at close range the Messerschmitt caught fire and then just blew up right in front of Yellow 2. Hughes felt the jolt as his machine was hit, and looking round found a dangerous looking Me109 on his tail. Tightening his turn, he pulled his Spitfire (R6896) inside the 109 which immediately began to climb away in front of him. As it began to move through his gunsight, Hughes opened fire, blasting pieces from behind the 109's cockpit. It caught fire, nosed over and crashed into the sea.

Four Ju87 dive-bombers went by him, heading south and he closed in to make an attack but as he opened fire, a 109 sliced in behind him, its bullets slamming into the Spitfire's tailplane. The Spitfire dived, with its trimming tabs shot away, but Hughes regained control as the 109 overshot him. He lined up on the Messerschmitt but hardly had he pressed the gun button than his guns fell silent – he was out of ammunition. One lucky 109 pilot headed south and away.

Joe O'Brien, following his arrival, led the squadron at 2.20 pm on the 18th (in P9466); Hughes led Blue Section (in X4036). A married man with a young daughter, O'Brien was to tread the same path with destiny as his Australian flight commander. They flew over the Isle of Wight at 16,000 feet, when about twenty Me109s appeared above them in the sun. Hughes climbed towards them, his section making individual attacks. His own first attack on a 109 from 150 yards, produced no visible results, then he became too busy when a couple of 109s turned their attention to him, and did not see the 109 again. One of the two Messerschmitts opened fire at him from extreme range; Hughes turned to attack this machine, his first burst setting the 109 on fire. The German's companion attacked the Australian, climbed away and then began to dive. Hughes was after it in an instant, chasing it until the 109 pilot started to pull up, then he let go two two-second bursts from 30 yards. With his aircraft mortally hit, the German pilot jumped, parachuting down onto the island, followed by his crashing fighter plane. Hughes circled, watching, seeing another cloud of smoke and fire rising a short way off which appeared to be the remains of the first 109 he had shot down.

Leading the squadron in the late afternoon of 26 August, Hughes was ordered to the Portsmouth area just before 5 pm. Hughes was now flying Spitfire X4009 in which he was to fly for the remainder of his time in action. Above Portsmouth they intercepted eight red-nosed Me109s flying at 16,000 feet, with a further thirty 109s some 2,000 feet above and three miles away. Hughes led his section down in line astern on the leading eight who saw the danger and· immediately split up into sections of two. Hughes went for the leading two 109s, firing a five-second burst at the rear one which burst into flames and dropped vertically. The leading Messerschmitt immediately began to climb but then turned to dive away. It caught a long burst from the Australian's eight guns as it began to pull out and started to burn. The German pilot stayed with his burning fighter for several minutes as he headed out to sea, then took to his parachute above what seemed to Hughes to be an auxiliary motor launch painted dark grey and blue. As Hughes flew low to look at the vessel it opened fire at him, moving towards the German pilot who had meantime splashed down into the water. Hughes left them to it and headed back to the English coast. On the way, three 109s saw him, one making a quick pass, firing from 1,000 yards. With empty guns Hughes flew off and returned to Wallop.

Hughes had now destroyed, including shared kills, a total of nine German aircraft, having scored double victories in his last three combats. In his next scrap he got three!

This occurred on 4 September. Hughes led the squadron on patrol at 12.50 pm and when above Tangmere at 10,000 feet saw about fifty twin-engined Me110s approaching the English coast with a further fifteen flying further north just south of Hazelmere.

Ordering Red, Yellow and Green Sections to tackle the approaching Germans, he took Blue Section towards the northerly group of fifteen. These 110s quickly formed a defensive circle when they saw the Spitfires, but like others had discovered before him, Hughes knew that the best way to attack this type of defensive manoeuvre was to fly against the circle in the opposite direction – and from head-on! He got in two short bursts at the leading 110, then pulled up to fire another burst into its fuselage. The Messerschmitt caught fire and hit the ground just north of Brighton. Already he had pounced on a second 110, but this time from behind, the circle having been broken. This 110 rolled over onto its back, dived vertically to the ground where it blew up ten miles north of Tangmere.

It was now time for him to be the target. Three 110s attacked him while others circled around his Spitfire. Hughes snapped off three short bursts to break up the deadly circle and one of the Messerschmitts broke and dived away. Hughes was after it like a cat after a rat, emptying his guns, and he saw one engine catch fire. The 110 pilot headed towards the South Coast, now with smoke coming from both engines. It flew lower and lower but before it hit the water Hughes saw a Hurricane fire a short burst into it. Hughes landed back at base exactly one hour after take-off, having increased his personal score by three.

*

The very next day, in the afternoon, Hughes was hammering the Luftwaffe fighters again. Leading his Blue Section off with the rest of the squadron at 2.45 pm, he was following Red Section at 20,000 feet going towards Gravesend where exploding anti-aircraft fire was staining the summer blue sky. They had been up an hour and were quite near Eastchurch when suddenly three Me109s came hurtling down from the glare of the sun. As a warning yell was given, and Hughes rapidly hauled his Spitfire round, he saw two 'Vee' formations of 109s flying up the Thames Estuary, the first of five aeroplanes, the second of seven. Joined equally suddenly by two Hurricanes, Hughes turned and dived.

A dog-fight ensued right above Eastchurch. Hughes fired a full deflection shot at one Messerschmitt which hit its ammunition bays. The German fighter exploded and went down in a spin shedding bits and pieces. Three 109s curved upwards; Hughes circled, then attacked the rear one which separated from the others. He chased it, firing from dead astern; his bullets shattered the German's oil tank, for oil sprayed back to cover his wings. The 109, mortally hit, planed down to force-land in a field about fifteen miles south-west of Manston aerodrome. One account states the German pilot to have been Franz von Werra of JG3 who later gained fame by successfully escaping from captivity in Canada, being the subject of the book and the film entitled *The One That Got Away*. However, if Hughes' estimation of the place the 109 landed was correct, von Werra came to rest in a field near Winchet Hill, south of Maidstone. This is considerably further than fifteen miles from Manston. Also, according to the book, von Werra came down around 10 am in the morning. Hughes noted in his combat report that the twelve 109s each had red-noses with the others had white spinners with black and white camouflage – more probably dark and light shades of grey.

As the pace continued, Hughes was off again at 8.40 am the next morning as Cressy Blue Leader. Fifty minutes later, whilst at 24,000 feet in the Dover area, Hughes spotted enemy fighters below and led his section down towards them. There were twenty-five Me109s and he fired a long burst into one of them from 150 yards to 50 yards, and it went down rapidly and crashed on landing about five miles west of Littlestone. Climbing back to 10,000 feet he intercepted five 109s escorting an Me110 high across Dover harbour. This 110 had one engine on fire and just as it cleared Dover the crew baled out and the 110 fell into the sea.

Hughes came in behind the rearmost Messerschmitt, firing another long burst but then three 109s dived on him from the beam. He just had time to fire a second burst into the 109, emptying his guns, being rewarded by having his wings and windscreen splattered in oil. Breaking away to attack the other 109s he discovered his guns were empty so broke off the action. The last he saw of the second 109 was it smoking badly and losing height. He was credited with a probable.

This brought his score to 15 and 1 probable, 12 of these and the probable being claimed in just three weeks but actually in only seven combats. His reward of a single DFC seems little by comparison. Apart from the three earlier Ju88s, all his subsequent victories had been over German fighters, 9 (10 including the probable) over the nimble and highly dangerous Me109E single-seaters.

Yet, like so many others before, and after him, this gallant and aggressive Australian's luck deserted him the very next afternoon. It was the day the Luftwaffe first attacked London. Led by his CO, Joe O'Brien, who had himself accounted for four German aircraft plus one probable since taking command of 234 Squadron on 17 August, Hughes and the others scrambled at 5.35 pm. Still flying in X4009, and O'Brien in his P9466, they climbed towards their enemies in the afternoon sky. At approximately 6 o'clock between London and the seaside town of Brighton, and at heights varying between 25,000 to 30,000 feet, they found them.

Two-three-four Squadron were initially ordered to patrol over Kenley and Biggin Hill aerodromes at Angels 10 (10,000 feet) but O'Brien led them to 20,000 feet on arriving over their patrol area to find scores of enemy bombers and fighters streaming southwards. The Germans were on their way home, being harried and hit from all sides. O'Brien ordered Hughes to go for the bombers while he covered them with his section, so Hughes winged over and then dived towards a group of Dornier 17s.

O'Brien's Red Section was attacked by yellow-nosed Me109s. O'Brien was hit and killed; his Number Two was engaged by another 109 with a white spinner, but he escaped. It was noticeable in this action that the German fighter formations were heavier than those previously met over Southern England.

Meanwhile, Hughes closed right in to make a quarter attack on a straggling Dornier which had dropped slightly behind and below the German formation. His Number Two saw Hughes firing and blasting large chunks off the enemy bomber; then its wing crumpled and the Dornier went into a fatal and irrevocable spin towards the English countryside. But his 'get in close' technique became the instrument of his downfall. Whether it was part of the Dornier's wing or another large object it is not certain, but something flew back and smashed into one of the Australian's wings and Blue Two saw the Spitfire go spinning down after the Dornier with about one third of its wing broken, to crash. He hit the ground just seconds after his sixteenth kill and died instantly.

Fighting his King's enemies half way around the world from his native land the blazing meteor that was P.C. Hughes was suddenly extinguished.

11

Willie

Like father, like son. How often has this been said? With the two World Wars only twenty years apart there were, of course, many men who fought in the Great War of 1914-18 whose sons had to take arms against Germany during the second conflict of 1939-45. The, like father, like son, applied to many of these, but none more so than to William Bernard Rhodes Moorhouse (no hyphen at this stage[1]) and his son William Henry Rhodes-Moorhouse.

William senior was born on 26 September 1887, the second child (of four) of Edward and Mary Moorhouse. He was educated at Harrow and Cambridge, and even from his early youth he was always keenly interested in all manner of speed. Motor cycles, motor cars and racing took up much of his formative years, so it was natural that one such as he should turn to the new dimension of flight as this became popular in the early 1900's. He learnt to fly at his own expense and even began designs for a monoplane. He quickly established himself as an able and competitive pilot, even travelling to the United States to take part in early flying race meetings as well as flying demonstration flights.

William married in 1912, and his son William Henry was born in 1914. When later that year the First World War began, he immediately joined the Royal Flying Corps and in March 1915 joined No 2 Squadron in France, flying the BE2 aeroplanes. When the First Battle of Ypres erupted on 22 April, 2 Squadron was detailed to fly bombing missions against German lines of communication. Three days later, on the 25th, Rhodes Moorhouse left his base at Merville, to bomb Courtrai railway station. He dropped his 100 lb bomb but in flying through a veritable wall of small arms fire his BE was hit and he himself was badly wounded.

[1] W.B. Moorhouse had to take the name of Rhodes to enable him to succeed to the estate of his grandfather.

His thigh was ripped open but instead of landing immediately to receive treatment, and captivity, he chose to fly back to the British lines. Flying fairly low he was fired on by all manner of German ground troops and positions, being wounded twice more, one bullet opening his abdomen, another going through his hand. He flew some 30 miles, landed back at his base and insisted on giving a full report before allowing anyone to take him to the local Casualty Clearing Station for medical assistance. He survived until the 27th when he finally succumbed to his wounds. For his gallantry and devotion to duty he was awarded the Victoria Cross – the first airman ever to receive Britain's highest award for personal bravery. His body was returned to the family home at Parnham, Dorset, for burial.

*

His young son William, also known as Willie to most of his friends and relatives, had, not unnaturally, a similar interest in flying and from a personal standpoint, inherited many of his father's mannerisms. He too lived to enjoy speed, danger and excitement. He also enjoyed sport and the outdoor life. Ski-ing holidays in Switzerland, with, what would today be called the jet-set, and sporting holidays in Cornwall all helped to develop the young Rhodes-Moorhouse.

After preparatory school, Willie went to Eton College and during a school holiday to Switzerland, made friends with G.W.S 'Mouse' Cleaver, whose mother owned her own private aeroplane. She took Willie for a flight which in turn led him to take an even keener interest in flight, and to learn to fly himself. Willie's mother then bought him his own aeroplane, a De Havilland Moth. This later led Willie to join 601 Auxiliary Squadron, which was more like a social flying club full of friends than an auxiliary fighter unit. All its pilots were more or less well-to-do and most owned their own private aeroplanes. One of his fellow pilots was the same Mouse Cleaver.[1]

In 1936 Willie married Amalia Demetriadi, daughter of Sir Stephen.[2]

[1] Mouse Cleaver was badly wounded on 15 August 1940.

[2] Her brother Richard Demetriadi, also in 601 Squadron, was killed on 11 August 1940.

Willie Rhodes-Moorhouse

When the Second World War began, Willie Rhodes-Moorhouse and 601 Squadron, were immediately mobilized. It was equipped with Gloster Gauntlet biplanes but soon after war was declared it re-equipped with twin-engined Bristol Blenheim fighters.

One early problem the adventurous pilots of 601 discovered as wartime petrol rationing came in, was how to continue running their various modes of personal transport – mostly fast motor cycles. Rhodes-Moorhouse was made petrol officer and told to solve the problem. He solved it all right – he went out and bought a local garage!

On 27 November, six Blenheims of the squadron, led by Michael Peacock, joined six Blenheims of 25 Squadron in a joint venture – an attack upon the German seaplane base at Borkum, in the Heligoland Bight, a journey of 250 miles. Willie was one of the 601 pilots chosen to go. They arrived over the German base at dusk, having just flown through a rainstorm, taking the Germans completely by surprise. They thoroughly shot up the target, hitting five seaplanes on slipways, damaging several patrol boats and raking hangars. The defences had hardly time to reply when it was all over and every single Blenheim flew out unscathed. Peacock won the DFC, one of the first awarded in WW2, for his part in the raid but died in France commanding a fighter unit in May 1940.

*

In the early months of 1940, 601's flyers ferried aircraft out to France, then in March they converted to single-seat Hawker Hurricane fighters. By May, when the Germans launched their attack in the west, 601 was operational on the new type and ready for anything. Then the unit was moved to Hawkinge near the south coast.

The Battle of France was going badly – the Armies of Britain and France falling back ahead of the German onslaught. In the air too the RAF and French Air Force were outnumbered and being constantly overwhelmed. Thus, on 17 May, the flights of 601 took it in turns to fly over to France, being temporarily attached to support the Allied Expeditionary Force. Willie Rhodes-Moorhouse went – to the very airfield at Merville from where, twenty-five years earlier, his father had flown to win his Victoria Cross.

The very next afternoon, the 18th, Willie and B Flight went on patrol over Brussels at 8,000 feet. When east of the Belgium capital they found twelve Heinkel 111s flying in pairs just above and in and out of 8/10ths cloud. In the attack Rhodes-Moorhouse fired at one from 300 down to 200 yards, which produced a lot of black smoke from one engine. Then the Heinkel whipped into a steep right-hand turn, then dived earthwards. Victory number one came at the cost of several bullets in his Hurricane, one going right through his oil tank.

On the following afternoon 601 patrolled between Douai and Cambrai when they ran into fifty Heinkels escorted by Me110 fighters. The bombers were in three waves, flying south; 601 met them while flying in the opposite direction, 2,000 feet above.

Sweeping round in a curve, the British pilots waded in. Rhodes-Moorhouse was attacking Heinkels on the starboard side when his eye caught sight of four or five Messerschmitts coming in from the right. He heaved his Hurricane round and flew right through the 110s, firing as he went. The 110s fired back; bullets slashed into his machine, hitting his fuel tank which caused petrol to pour into his cockpit. Quickly he dived away vertically, levelling out at 50 feet near Cambrai, which he could see clearly being bombed. He finally landed at Abbeville, refuelled, then flew back to RAF Manston.

He was quickly back in action, and at 7.35 am on the 22nd, 601 fought some Me109s south-east of St Omer. A dog-fight began when the two formations met, Rhodes-Moorhouse finding himself suddenly alone. Seeing some aircraft 2,000 feet above, he climbed thinking they were Hurricanes, only to discover them to be Messerschmitts. In seconds he found himself going round in a tight right-hand turn with three Me109s. On the second time round he found himself right on the tail of one Messerschmitt. His first two short bursts missed the turning target but the third scored; the 109 dived down and away in a right-hand spiral with smoke pouring from it.

*

One amusing story concerns Willie and 601 at the end of May 1940. Nine Hurricanes were required to escort a Flamingo aeroplane from Warmwell to Paris. On arrival at Villacoublay, Paris, the passenger proved to be none other than Mr Winston Churchill, the Prime Minister. Churchill was in France to talk with the French Premier.

Due to the length of the meeting, the nine pilots from 601 were released, and they quickly decided on a night in the French capital. The following morning, according to Major General Sir Edward Spears, the nine Hurricanes and the Flamingo stood ready as the Prime Minister walked to his aeroplane, waving his stick and having a few words with the fighter escort. Spears watched as the pilot's faces lit up and smiled, looking like 'the angels of my childhood'. In his book, *Assignment to Catastrophe Vol II*, Spears was intrigued by their angelic looks, their handsome faces, confident and inspiring.

Yet, according to Mouse Cleaver, one of the nine, the pilots were hung-over, unshaven, dirty and smelly, and when Churchill arrived, Rhodes-Moorhouse was being sick behind his Hurricane. Hardly a promise for the future, but Churchill nevertheless, spoke to them, apparently accepting their appearance without comment. It had been a great night in Paris!

With the final collapse in France, 601 and the other RAF units had to evacuate, returning to England, tired, but more than ready to continue the fight.

The fight continued for Rhodes-Moorhouse on 7 July. His section was scrambled after a hostile, finding and chasing a Dornier 17P of 2(F)/121. When they spotted the German, the Hurricanes went into line astern, the normal tactic at this period of the war. Willie, on the right of the formation behind the section leader, was showered with empty cartridge cases as the leader opened fire, one shell-case chipping his windscreen. As the leader broke away, the Dornier began to dive down to 100 feet above the sea. Rhodes-Moorhouse followed, firing continuously until he lost the bomber momentarily. When he saw it again it was being finished off by Green Section.

Four days later, on the 11th, Willie was scrambled again, climbing hard over the Isle of Wight, the scene of so much action. Heading out to sea, he and his wingman spotted another Dornier 17P (identified as a Do215 by the two RAF pilots) in the sun about ten to fifteen miles away. Closing with it, Rhodes-Moorhouse had some difficulty in making sure it was a German until he got in really close. Once he was satisfied he attacked, seeing his fire going right into the Dornier's fuselage. His wingman, Pilot Officer J.W.

Bland, also attacked. The German then dived vertically towards the sea, flattening out at 500 feet. Willie attacked again, as it continued to lose height down to 100 feet. Very soon afterwards the Dornier appeared to be flying one wing low; then it hit the sea, sinking immediately, twenty miles out to sea at 10.14 am.

*

The last combat for Willie Rhodes-Moorhouse during the Channel battles occurred on 16 July. He was leading Blue Section, leaving the ground at 4.40 pm in the afternoon. Only eighteen minutes later they saw a Ju88A of II/KG54. It was flying at 9,000 feet, just above a mass of 9/10ths cloud, towards the west end of the Solent. He attacked and his fire shattered the German's starboard engine, and its propeller suddenly stood stark and still. The bomber went into a shallow dive heading southwards. He called for assistance when his ammunition was finished but the Junkers was already mortally hit, and as he watched, it dropped into the sea at 5.05 pm. A yellow dinghy bobbed to the surface and two of the German crew clambered into it. In company with Green Leader, Willie circled the two survivors, and then he flew to and fro, attracting the attention of a rescue boat which eventually picked them up. They then flew home, an hour after the 88 went down.

On 11 August the Luftwaffe attacked in force and 601 Squadron was in the air during the mid-morning. Willie led the squadron and Blue Section, with Red and Green Sections on his right and left respectively, while Yellow Section flew 'in the box'. The squadron was ordered to patrol St Catherine's Point at a height of 20,000 feet, then told to patrol over Portland.

This was the period when German sweeps of Me109s were proving dangerous to Fighter Command's hard pressed fighters; Air Vice Marshal Keith Park was trying hard to prevent his valuable Spitfires and Hurricanes from becoming mixed up with the Messerschmitts. However, in the fight which developed over Portland on the 11th, 601 did tangle with German fighters.

At 10.30 am, when twenty miles south of Swanage, they saw a large armada of Me109s and Me110s in layers between 15 and 25,000 feet. 601 was at 19,000 feet when they saw them, Rhodes-Moorhouse recorded that there was 'too many (EA) to estimate'. The German fighters were milling around to the south, so 601

Hurricanes landing at Biggin Hill (32 Squadron) on 15 August 1940.

turned towards them. As he turned, his engine spluttered and stopped, so Willie told the others to keep going without him. As he dropped out of formation, he discovered that he had been flying on his reserve tank which had emptied. This was dangerous for it now left an empty tank full of petrol fumes right in front of him. An incendiary bullet in that and ...! Quickly changing over to the main tank he climbed again but in those few moments, he lost sight of the rest of the squadron.

Still grabbing height, three Me109s appeared on his left and attacked him but Willie saw them and turned to meet the threat. They came towards each other head-on, both sides firing. Flashing by each other, Willie passing just below the 109s, he made a very sharp left-hand turn and spun down to 14,000 feet, successfully losing his new found 'friends'.

Rhodes-Moorhouse hauled his fighter up to 25,000 feet above the huge gaggle of 109s and began to circle them. All he could see was Messerschmitts, not a single RAF machine anywhere. The 109s were circling around in sections of three to five in lines astern at various heights. Willie dived across the mass of 109s, firing as he went, as and when a target presented itself. He hit at least one Messerschmitt but had no idea if it crashed or not. Climbing again he then turned to make another attack from the opposite direction. This time he went for a section of three 109s from astern, firing at the leader but he did not allow enough deflection and missed. However, his shots hit the two 109s following the leader, one going down in flames, the other nose-diving away in a steep dive. Rhodes-Moorhouse watched them fall, both splashing into the sea below.

Until now, the 109 pilots seemed so intent on watching each other, that Willie's Hurricane appeared to go unnoticed. But with the loss of two of their comrades they became only too aware of his unwanted presence, and four 109s peeled off to attack him. Believing he was now low on ammunition, Willie half rolled and dived away to safety. When he landed he found he had fired 300 rounds from each of seven guns with 100 rounds from the eighth, the latter having a broken retaining pawl spring.

During this action, 601's other pilots had been engaged by Me109s, four of the British flyers having been shot down and killed over Portland. It was a severe blow.

Exactly one week later, on 18 August, Rhodes-Moorhouse fought another hectic but successful action. It was a busy day for the RAF, casualties on both sides being heavy. It was also the day the infamous Stuka dive-bombers received a severe mauling by defending RAF fighters.

Blue Section led by Willie, who also led the squadron, were scrambled at 1.35 pm; the squadron only had ten Hurricanes available. With Red and Green Sections on either side of him he led them up as fast as he could. Levelling out at 12,000 feet above their base airfield, Control then ordered them south to Selsey Bill. The Luftwaffe was on its way in.

Rhodes-Moorhouse led the Hurricanes across Selsey from the west, seeing a horde of German aircraft to his left, heading in from the south about five miles out to sea. He estimated a force of more than fifty, headed by two formations of Ju87s, twenty in each, flying in a close vic. Stepped up in line astern were about twenty Messerschmitts above and to the sides. It was just 2 pm.

Over the R/T, Willie ordered his men into lines astern, then turning to starboard dived upon the rear formation of Ju87s, making a head-on attack from their starboard bow. 43 Squadron flying nearby also attacked. Willie opened fire as he approached, then sped over them, but saw no results from his fire. Passing quickly and upwards he immediately became embroiled with Me109s but Willie snapped off short bursts at several from both head-on and turning onto their tails. He hit more than one but only one did he actually see go down and crash, having no chance to see the results of his other bursts. He dog-fought these 109s until his guns were empty, landing back at base at 2.30 pm.

Number 601 Squadron, once again led by Rhodes-Moorhouse, blasted a Heinkel 111H from III/KG27 in the late afternoon of 30 August off the south coast. It was flown by Oberleutnant Hunerbein, who, with his crew, were taken prisoner. The next day Rhodes-Moorhouse was in action again.

It was yet another action-packed day and 601 were heavily involved. Once again he led the squadron with his Blue Section, scrambling from Debden just before 1 o'clock. Having grabbed 10,000 feet of valuable height over the Thames Estuary and when just east of Tilbury, Willie spotted enemy aircraft off to his left flying towards Tilbury, 5,000 feet higher than the Hurricanes. There were two formations of Dornier 17s, each consisting of two vics of six machines, supported by a large number of Me109 fighters flying several thousand feet above and in section of three in line astern.[1]

Willie Rhodes-Moorhouse headed the squadron to the left, climbing above the Dorniers, but then his section was engaged by three 109s. He managed to shake them off then headed again towards the bombers but before closing the range, was engaged again by three more Messerschmitts. He pulled round firing at one which had gone into a vertical bank right in front of him, 60 to 70 yards away. His burst shattered the Messerschmitt's hood, which sprinkled away like glistening crystal as the 109 went into a right-hand vertical dive. Willie had no time to watch its fall as he headed again for the Dorniers. They were now some distance away but again the defensive tactics by the 109s proved effective, for they cut him off. Surrounded by deadly Messerschmitts, Willie lined up one as it raced towards him head-on, fired and yanked his Hurricane round in a screaming turn to follow. The 109 was hit and spun away with smoke pouring out but again he could not see it fall because of the close proximity of other 109s. With empty guns he quickly broke off the fight, said a last farewell to the disappearing Dorniers and headed for home. Following this fight he was credited with two Me109s probably destroyed.

Willie's last successful combat occurred on 4 September at 1.30 pm in the afternoon. He was yet again leading the squadron, patrolling Debden at 10,000 feet before being ordered towards the south coast. Still gaining height, the Hurricane pilots saw a large formation of German aeroplanes, about ten to fifteen miles to the east and north of Worthing, flying southwards at 12,000 feet. Willie led his men up to 13,000 feet heading south-east to intercept them at the coast with the sun behind them.

Rhodes-Moorhouse identified the hostile machines as Dornier 17s, but it is more likely they were Me110s. Ordering his pilots into line astern, he attacked, and then the battle broke up into individual dog-fights. The German machine Willie attacked broke away from

[1] Quite often in RAF combat reports, British pilots refer to seeing enemy fighters flying in threes, sometimes fives. It is well known that Luftwaffe 109s flew in pairs and fours. Obviously the RAF took it that some of their opponents flew similar formations to the RAF who flew in sections of three.

the others in a steep left hand turn. Despite fire from the rear gunner, mostly inaccurate, Willie continued his attack, knocking-out the enemy gunner just as the machine turned onto its back to dive towards the sea. Just above the water it levelled out, still flying south, but leaving a trail of smoke from its port engine. Making another stern quarter attack the German finally gave up the fight and crashed into the sea fifteen miles south of Worthing.

*

The gallant and well-loved Willie Rhodes-Moorhouse, recently awarded the DFC, was killed in action over Kent at around 9.30 am on the morning of 6 September 1940. He was flying Hurricane P8818. Three pilots of the squadron went down at that time during a fight with Messerschmitt 109s. One pilot baled out but Rhodes-Moorhouse and another veteran, Flying Officer C.R. Davis DFC (a South African flying P3363) who himself had shot down some ten German aircraft, about the same number as Willie had claimed were both killed.

Willie's Hurricane was seen to emerge from a mass of twisting and turning aeroplanes above Tonbridge, fall vertically and plunge into the ground. His body was recovered, cremated, and then his mortal ashes were interred next to his father's grave at Parnham. Like father, like son, the two flyers of different wars remain at peace beneath a Dorset sky.

*

Willie Rhodes-Moorhouse had been the star turn in 601 Squadron. His portrait was drawn by Captain Cuthbert Orde, and in Orde's book, the great artist wrote:

> It is true to say that his loss affected the whole squadron from the CO to the humblest aircraftman. They couldn't believe it – it just couldn't have happened. His extraordinary combination of gaiety, *joie de vivre*, personal attraction and fighting qualities was something that just didn't disappear suddenly.

Max Aitken, who had also flown in 601 Squadron said to Orde, 'When Willie was killed the aggressive spirit went out of the squadron.'

12

John

On 28 November, 1940, 609 Squadron, the Royal Air Force and England, lost one one of its most brilliant young men, who would undoubtedly been of great benefit to his country, if not the world, had he survived the war, or if indeed the world had, in 1939, managed to avoid the senseless recourse to war as a solution to its problems. John Charles Dundas, a Yorkshireman, tall, good-looking with a brilliant mind and amusing personality, simply disappeared in the autumn sky, in the highly dangerous autumn sky, off the Isle of Wight on that November day.

John Dundas, also known to his friends as 'Dogs', was an aristocrat, related to two Yorkshire families, the Marquis of Zetland, and Viscount Halifax. At twelve years of age he won a scholarship to Stowe, then won a place at Christ Church, Oxford at seventeen, where he gained a First in Modern History. Following this he studied at the Sorbonne in Paris and later at Heidelberg University. He became a specialist in foreign affairs, especially European matters, even being part of Neville Chamberlain's entourage to Rome at the time of Munich in 1938.

Dundas the intellectual became a journalist on the editorial staff of the *Yorkshire Post* newspaper, but in his spare time, he learned to fly with 609 Auxiliary Air Force Squadron, at Yeadon. When Europe was plunged into war in 1939, Dundas and 609 Squadron were very soon ready to help defend their country against the might of the German Luftwaffe.

*

Number 609 Squadron went into the front line during the Dunkirk evacuation, flying their first war patrol on 30 May. It was not an auspicious beginning, for no enemy aircraft were seen and due to less than favourable weather; one pilot was killed in a crash and Yellow Section, (Flight Lieutenant F.J. Howell, Flying Officer J.

John Dundas

Dawson and Flying Officer J.C. Dundas) lost its way. With rapidly drying fuel tanks, Howell got down at Rochford while Dundas and Dawson both force-landed at Friston, Dundas damaging his mainplane.

The next day, however, was more successful. Ordered to rendezvous at North Weald at 12.30 pm, they stood-by at '30 minutes availability'. At two o'clock 609 took off for a patrol over Dunkirk at 20,000 feet. In a brief skirmish, two German aircraft were shot up and one flight commander lost. On the next patrol, Dundas (flying L1096) and the others attacked several bombers over the sea. Three Heinkel 111s and a Dornier 17, as well as two Me109s were claimed, one Heinkel falling to Dundas. He also knocked pieces from a Dornier. One pilot was lost and another came down in the sea but was rescued.

When the Channel battles commenced, 609 had moved from Northolt to Middle Wallop (following a brief stay at Warmwell). On 13 July John Dundas led Yellow Section (Pilot Officer R.F.G. Miller and Pilot Officer C.N. Overton) to patrol over a convoy. They failed to locate the ships but did find a large gaggle of German aeroplanes flying at 15,000 feet near Portland. Dundas (in R6634) and Miller (L1065) climbed above them, (Overton in L1082 dropping out with engine trouble) and attacked out of the sun. Dundas hammered one Me110 which fell away to be claimed as destroyed but in fact it returned home although it was damaged. Dundas was then heavily engaged by several 110s and had to break off the fight and land at Warmwell. Miller found another 110, dog-fought it then fired at a Dornier which then was finished off by 238 Squadron. Dundas' Me110 came from V/LG1; its pilot, Leutnant Krebitz, was wounded.

The records of 609 show that Dundas and Overton had a similar engagement on 19 July and that again 238 Squadron was also involved with the enemy. However, this might be a duplicated report for certainly no such losses appear from the German side. Meantime, Dundas had had a narrow escape during a night flying practice sortie. Coming into land he hit a Bofors gun, damaging it and his Spitfire, also smashing several paraffin flares but luckily he got away without injury.

*

As we read in the chapter on David Crook, 609 Squadron were in action daily between 11 and 14 August, and of course John Dundas was in the thick of it as well.

On the first day, the 11th, he flew R6769, taking off at 9.45 am, leading his Yellow Section. Ten miles south-west of the Isle of Wight at 24,000 feet, Dundas lost sight of the squadron. Continuing to fly south he found nine Hurricanes, but by now they were all in mid-Channel so he decided to head back. As he made a wide sweeping turn he saw white smoke trails above him and to the left. Putting his two wingmen into line astern, he circled in a wide climbing turn. As he gained height he saw a great number of Messerschmitt 110s circling in a fairly tight left hand turn and above them he felt sure were a number of single-seater Me109s.

Gaining a position above the 110s he led his small band down (or so he imagined, but in fact he became separated from the other two and attacked alone), selected a 110 and opened fire. The Messerschmitt went sharply to the left in a climbing turn. Dundas whirled after it, closing right into point blank range, then gave the German a two-second burst, breaking away when it seemed certain he would collide with it. He had seen his bullets chew into the Messerschmitt's fuselage but nothing really definite.

Meanwhile the 110's rear gunners were providing excellent defensive crossfire and Dundas' Spitfire was hit and damaged. Dundas ignored this, sticking with his 110, and still in a left-hand climbing turn, gave it a full deflection burst from 250 to 100 yards, giving it a four-second raking. Smoke issued from both the 110's engines, then it staggered and fell over to the left. As Dundas broke away, more bullets went through his starboard wing and rudder. However, the 110 was finished and it went down, and like David Crook, Dundas was credited with one of the several Me110s of I/ZG2 brought down over Swanage that Sunday morning.

The next day, in N3113, Dundas was away at mid-day, leading his section against 60-plus Me110s and Me109s off the east coast of the Isle of Wight. Dundas followed Red Section into the attack, picking a 110 to fire a two-second burst into it from 300 to 100 yards. Bits flew off of the German's wing and its starboard engine burst into flames. Dundas broke vertically downwards through layers of circling 110s then hauled his Spitfire back up again. Making another attack on the Messerschmitts he met one head-on, both pilots firing at each other as the gap betwen them closed. No result – and again Dundas broke downwards. As he tried to repeat his method of climbing up to make yet another attack, a red-nosed Me109 came screaming down but fired wildly, and Dundas easily shook it off. Re-claiming the precious height above the mass of 110s, Dundas saw a gap in the circle and latched onto the tail of one and fired a long five-second burst from right behind it. Smoke began to trail from both engines but other 110s were closing in and low on ammunition Dundas called it a day and flew home. These 110s might have again been from ZG2 or ZG76, both units losing aircraft over the south coast of England at the time of 609's action.

Day three, the 13th, The Germans' *Adler Tag* – Eagle Day, Dundas found himself as spare pilot when 609 was scrambled at 3.30 pm, so he latched himself as Number Four in Red Section, flying R6690.

Breaking through and above cloud at 10,000 feet, Dundas quickly spotted German fighters high above. Red Leader could not see them so he instructed Dundas to take over the lead. Climbing into the sun, they reached 18,000 feet but then below he saw three large vic formations of Stuka dive-bombers silhouetted against the clouds below, flying north. Red Leader, the CO, took over the lead, then led his squadron down; Dundas re-slotted himself in the Number Four position. Then he watched as the first three pilots of Red Section went down on the rear three Ju87s from out of the sun – the Germans taking no evasive action and all three dive-bombers heeled over and went down under the Spitfires' guns.

Dundas slid down behind the starboard Junkers of the next section to port, opening fire at 250 yards but with too much overtaking speed, had to rapidly throttle back. Steadying at point-blank range he let go a four-second burst, seeing his gull-winged target erupt in a sheet of flame and fall into the clouds. Turning, he went down on another Stuka which was already under assault by other Spitfires. Waiting his turn, he found himself too close and was only able to get in a quick burst before he all but collided with it. Then a bullet from one or other of the rear-gunners punctured his Spitfire's oil system. He broke off the action and dropped down with no oil pressure, force-landing at Warmwell with a dead prop. The Stukas came from II/StG2.

Just over twenty-four hours later, John Dundas was patrolling above Boscombe Down at 15,000 feet in R6961, having climbed through 10/10ths cloud. Shortly after reporting his position to control, he saw a twin-engined machine approaching from head-on. At first it looked like a British bomber, a Blenheim, until it was right beneath him, then Dundas saw the black and white crosses on its wings – it was a Messerschmitt 110. Dundas and his section were after it in a flash, Dundas getting off two bursts before the 110 dipped out of sight into the cloud.

Then the controller told him that two bandits were approaching his position at 15,000 feet. Climbing two thousand feet higher on his own he found four Dornier 17s in box formation, heading south towards the sea. As he saw them he also saw another Spitfire making attacks on them as they passed high over Salisbury. Closing to 800 yards and at 500 feet above the four German machines, Dundas made several attacks, each time aiming at the leading bomber. Then on his next attack he broke away too steeply and blacked out momentarily. Coming round, he found some difficulty in locating the bombers, but he did see them nearing the coast, the other Spitfire still nibbling at them, then it disappeared in cloud. Dundas caught up the bombers, selected the rear one, gave it a long six-second burst. The Dornier fell away from the formation and began to glide into cloud where he lost sight of it.

Returning northwards he then came up on a damaged Ju88 limping along and even as he closed, saw the wheels come down. Whether or not this was a sign of surrender or just the hydraulics failing, is not certain, but Dundas thought it just the result of battle damage and attacked. He fired off the rest of his ammunition into it which produced a puff of black smoke from its starboard motor. The Junkers went down and he watched until it crashed into a munitions store about five miles south-west of his own aerodrome, and broke up. Flight Lieutenant J.H.G. McArthur of 609 saw the 88 crash to confirm the kill.

For the third time Dundas's Spitfire had been hit by return fire, having a bullet hole through the airscrew and main-spar.

Apparently the Ju88 was in fact a Heinkel 111, the one attacked by David Crook, belonging to the Staff Staffel of KG55. This completed the fourth day of consecutive action in which 609 had been heavily engaged, and John Dundas had shot down a total of four German raiders, probably destroyed one and damaged two others. The next day, John's brother Hugh, serving with 616

(*Left*) John Dundas' brother Hugh who flew with 616 Squadron during the Battle.

(*Below*) Spitfire R6915 in the Imperial War Museum. Flown by several pilots in 609 Squadron, including John Dundas in October 1940. This machine destroyed five enemy aircraft, and damaged six others.

Squadron, shared in the destruction of a Ju88.[1]

Number 609 Squadron AAF had a tea-time party with a raid of 100-plus on 25 August, over Warmwell. The squadron's CO, Squadron Leader H.S. Darley, shot down the first German to fall. The bombers were Ju88s, but 609 was unable to get to them due to the aggressive defensive tactics employed by the Messerschmitt escort. However, 609 put in claims for 11 victories for the loss of two Spitfires, with one pilot wounded. The claims were a little optimistic, but they certainly destroyed several Me110s from II/ZG2 and V/ZG1, and Me109s of III/JG2. Dundas was credited with a 110 probably destroyed (R6769).

It was not until Sunday 15 September that John Dundas was able to make his next combat claim during a fight over London. In the first scrap of the day, (in R6922) Dundas damaged a Dornier 17. He saw the bombers and told his leader but receiving no orders, and seeing Me109s nearby, he decided to attack from below. He knocked-out one Dornier's engine but was then attacked by a 109 and later by three more.

Flying X4107, Dundas was off again that afternoon, leading his Yellow Section; his two wingmen were Pilot Officer Mike Appelby (R6631) and Pilot Officer V.C. 'Shorty' Keogh, an American (X4234). From high above Rye they saw a compact formation of 25 Dornier 17s heading south. 609, waiting for the returning raiders, went at them on the same level. Wading in, in line astern, behind Red Section, Dundas saw two Dorniers detach themselves from the main formation, attempting to dive away from the approaching trouble. Dundas selected one, already hit by other Spitfires, commenced firing at 300 yards down to 150, from behind and slightly above. Its rear-gunner fired back, twice hitting his Spitfire, but then his own fire began to chip pieces off the Dornier and flames streamed back from its wing and engine. As he broke away the Dornier spun down, its crew rapidly baling out, before it crashed into the sea. He received a share of that victory.

*

The September battles continued for John Dundas on the 24th,

[1] Later Group Captain H.S.L. Dundas DSO & bar, DFC. He was shot down by an Me109 on 22 August 1940 and wounded.

when 609 intercepted a raid on Swanage. Seated and strapped tight in X4472, Dundas enjoyed a dog-fight with a 110 in which he found he could easily hold the Messerschmitt's turn and climb inside it. Getting his sights on, he finally sent the German fighter spinning into the sea. He also damaged a Dornier in this action.

In the same Spitfire the next day, Dundas, with 609 in company, became embroiled in a huge air battle with over two hundred enemy aircraft shortly before noon. Heinkels and Dorniers in three distinct formations and escorted by at least thirty Me110s, were chased and caught south of Bristol. The city's AA fire, although well meant, was rather disturbing for the RAF pilots, but they waded in. 609 put in several claims, for one Spitfire damaged in return, Dundas claiming a Dornier. The Germans were so tightly packed together that it was almost impossible to be able to fire at individual aircraft, and Dundas was nearly hit by bombs falling from an aircraft above him.

It was just like early August again for 609, which was again in the thick of the action on four consecutive days, 24 to 27 September. On day three, the 26th, Dundas destroyed a Messerschmitt 109 and damaged a Dornier, then on the 27th, near Bristol shortly before mid-day, he got a 110. Unhappily the fighter controller positioned 609 so badly that they had little chance of getting through to the bombers. Added to this, both the flight commander's radio transmitters failed so Pilot Officer R.F.G. Miller, leading Yellow Section on this occasion, led 609 into the fighter escort circling above Warmwell, but Miller collided with a Messerschmitt and both machines exploded. As September ended, Dundas' personal score had topped the dozen mark.

*

The October battles with German fighters heralded the next phase of the RAF's conflict. For John Dundas, his first clash came on 7 October. Flying R6915 (the Spitfire now to be seen in the Imperial War Museum in London) as leader of Blue Section, he followed A Flight into about 15 Me110s, six miles to the north of Warmwell at 4.30 pm, part of a force attacking Yeovil. As usual the 110s went into their defensive circling game, Dundas flying straight across it, his eight guns rattling, but he could see no results. Hauling the Spitfire into a climb outside the circle he found a straggler which was without protection. After a short bout of turning, he latched onto the 110's tail and his thumb pressed against the gun button. Dundas let go a full 12-14 second burst into the Messerschmitt. Hit with this broadside, the 110's port motor began to stream smoke and coolant, then its starboard engine did likewise. The 110 pilot only tried moderate evasive action and Dundas closed right in for the kill, but was then hit by a cannon shell which exploded, sending shell splinters into his leg. The Spitfire went into a spin but Dundas recovered to land at Warmwell. The 110 was last seen at 14,000 feet just north of Weymouth with both engines out of action, but he only received credit for a probable.

Dundas hobbled to the station's sick quarters and in typical fashion was flying again the next day. The award of the DFC was announced two days later.

Nearly a week later, on the 15th, flying P9503, again as Blue Leader, Dundas was on patrol at 14,000 feet flying west over Christchurch. At least three vic formations of Me110s had flown over their heads some 5,000 feet above them, heading in a different direction. And above them, the RAF boys could see many Me109s. 609 began to climb to the south-west, trying to get to the Messerschmitt's height, but they became clearly silhouetted against 9/10ths white cumulus cloud which stretched below them like a carpet. It was then that David Crook, flying as Number Three to Dundas, yelled a warning, as three yellow-nosed Me109s came up from their starboard side below them. They had, evidently, just made an attack from above and astern of the section, their high speed placing them passed and below the Spitfires. Their surprise attack caused little damage; only one bullet hit Blue 2, but 609 broke up at the warning, and began to dive away in various directions.

Dundas tried to re-group B Flight at 12,000 feet, but without success as his radio transmitter began to fade. Instead he climbed alone, saw a gaggle of 15-20 Me110s at 18,000 feet and attacked. His first two passes, fired from 100 yards, produced no visible results and after each attack he had to break away steeply to avoid other enemy fighters above him. He was then chased for some time by two Me109s but he eventually lost them.

Later it was reported that an Me110 had crashed at Bournemouth. As Dundas had been the only pilot to attack enemy fighters above this locality, he was credited with it.[1] It was 609's 99th victory. Their 100th, a Ju88, was shot down by Flight Lieutenant Frankie Howell DFC and Pilot Officer Sydney Hill on 21 October. Hill's Spitfire, X4590, can be seen in the Battle of Britain Museum, Hendon, North London.

John Dundas was 609's leading pilot in terms of German aeroplanes brought down, his personal score now being 14 (including two shared), 3 probables plus a further 7 damaged. However, he had been lucky on several occasions, his various machines being hit and damaged on quite a number of sorties, and on 7 October when he had been slightly wounded, he had not even seen the Messerschmitt that had attacked him.

Nevertheless he was something of a tactician, always discussing the air fights with his colleagues, especially his new CO, Michael Robinson, in order to apply fresh ideas to the next action. He was regarded highly by all in 609, and well liked. Yet by now he was the last of the original 'A' (Auxiliary) pilots still with 609. These auxiliary airmen had a brass 'A' on each lapel of their dress uniform. As Hugh Dundas once described it, Regular airmen insisted that they stood for Amateur Airman, or even for 'Argue and Answer back' but all Auxiliaries wore their 'A's' with pride. Dundas had his own independent way of doing things, amply shown by his actions on 27 November, 1940.

Operations reported a Ju88 going home down the coast and Dundas requested permission to take a section up after it. Permission was refused, due no doubt to the belief that the German was well on his way. However, Dundas promptly asked if he could take up his section for a practice flight – which was granted! It was 1.40 pm.

Climbing eagerly and as fast as they could, they heard the controller report that the hostile would cross the coast at Southampton. Turning west, he spotted a line of shell bursts and looking beyond them he picked out a very small speck. It was the German flying south-west at 22,000 feet. The Spitfires began to give chase into the sun, using full throttle at 2,600 revs. The German was chased right across the Isle of Wight and the Channel but they only got close enough to identify it as a Junkers 88, when they

---

[1] It was also recorded as an Me109.

(*Right*) Major Helmut Wick, CO of JG2, shot down 28 November 1940.

(*Below*) Wick's Mc109E showing 42 of his eventual 57 victories.

approached the French coast, fifteen miles east of Cherbourg.

By now the Ju88 was reducing height, the Spitfires' speed being 280 mph, IAS. Dundas, in X4586, attacked at 14,000 feet having closed to 400 yards, when just off Cherbourg, letting go a five-second burst. The German rear-gunner put up a heavy and spirited return fire, but Dundas avoided it, opening fire again at 300, then 200 yards. His fire produced bright flashes off the German's fuselage and port wing, the port engine then beginning to smoke followed by a burst of flame. The Ju88 began to turn to port, then dived steeply. Dundas opened fire again as he curved after it, the 88 now diving in a steep left-hand spiral, out of control, smoke and flame streaming from its shattered engine.

Looking down, Dundas could now make out an airfield below, well stacked with Me109s, so decided to call it a day and flew home. He was credited with a probable. Not bad for a practice flight!

*

The next day, the 28th, was a very full day for the squadron. There were several alerts and scrambles against high flying Me109s, the last coming at 3.50 pm. Flight Lieutenant Dundas was again in X4586. In a battle with 109s in which Eric Marrs and 152 Squadron were also involved, there were several disjointed dog-fights near the Isle of Wight. Over the radio, the ground controller, Flight Lieutenant Fieldsend, heard John Dundas say, 'I've finished an Me109 – Whoopee!'

Squadron Leader Robinson replied, 'Good show, John,' after which nothing more was heard or seen of John Dundas or his Number Two, Pilot Officer P.A. Baillon (R6631). Baillon, a married man and former solicitor by profession, had been with 609 since September, and his wife was nearing the birth of their first child.

Initially it was hoped that Dundas had again gone chasing the Germans to France and been brought down on that side of the Channel but it was soon only too apparent that he had been shot down into the sea.

That evening the German Luftwaffe broadcast an appeal for information concerning the loss of one of their foremost fighter pilots, Major Helmut Wick, leader of Jagdgeschwader 2, and who had scored 56 victories.

There was a great deal of wishful thinking in 609 that it was John Dundas who had got the German 'ace' although seconds later Wick's pilots had probably got him and also Baillon. Whatever happened, one thing is certain, that the Royal Air Force and the Luftwaffe each lost one of their best pilots that cold November day. Two fighters who were very different to each other, Dundas the amateur week-end airman and intellectual, Wick the professional soldier and son of the Fatherland. It is the loss of such fine young men that brings no reason for the futility and waste of war.

John Dundas, whose award of a bar to his DFC was announced on Christmas Eve, 1940, had always achieved things without apparently trying too hard. In fact he achieved things by trying very hard but trying equally to seem not to be trying. In any event, the RAF and England lost a gallant son who would certainly have made his mark had he survived.

Appendix

The following list records the achievements of our twelve subjects in chronological order – and also the dates of their passing.

1939

17 Oct	FO H.P. Blatchford	He111	Destroyed (third share)

1940

18 May	FO W.H. Rhodes-Moorhouse	He111	Destroyed
22 May	FO W.H. Rhodes-Moorhouse	Me109	Destroyed
26 May	FL B.J.E. Lane	Ju87	Destroyed
		Me109	Destroyed
		Me109	Probable
31 May	FO J.C. Dundas	He111	Destroyed
		Do17	Destroyed
1 Jun	PO A.N.C. Weir	Me110	Destroyed
		Me109	Probable
1 Jun	FL B.J.E. Lane	Me110	Destroyed
		Do17	Damaged
18 Jun	WC F.V. Beamish	He111	Damaged
30 Jun	WC F.V. Beamish	2 Me109s	Destroyed
7 Jul	FO W.H. Rhodes-Moorhouse	Do17	Destroyed (third share)
8 Jul	FL P.C. Hughes	Ju88	Destroyed (third share)
9 Jul	PO D.M. Crook	Ju87	Destroyed
		Ju87	Damaged
9 Jul	WC F.V. Beamish	Me110	Destroyed (third share)
11 Jul	FO W.H. Rhodes-Moorhouse	Do17	Destroyed
12 Jul	WC F.V. Beamish	Do17	Destroyed (shared)
		Do17	Damaged
13 Jul	FO J.C. Dundas	Me110	Destroyed
13 Jul	PO D.M. Crook	Do17	Damaged
16 Jul	FO W.H. Rhodes-Moorhouse	Ju88	Destroyed
		Ju88	Damaged
18 Jul	PO A.N.C. Weir	He111	Destroyed (half share)
22 Jul	PO A.N.C. Weir	Do17	Destroyed (third share)
27 Jul	FL P.C. Hughes	Ju88	Destroyed (third share)
28 Jul	FL P.C. Hughes	Ju88	Destroyed (third share)
8 Aug	PO A.N.C. Weir	2 Me109s	Destroyed
		Ju87	Destroyed
11 Aug	PO D.M. Crook	Me110	Probable

11 Aug	FO J.C. Dundas	Me110	Destroyed
11 Aug	PO A.N.C. Weir – shot down near Christchurch – unhurt.		
12 Aug	PO D.M. Crook	2 Me109s	Destroyed
		Me110	Probable
12 Aug	FO J.C. Dundas	Me110	Destroyed
		Me110	Damaged
13 Aug	PO D.M. Crook	Me109	Destroyed
13 Aug	FO J.C. Dundas	Ju87	Destroyed
		Ju87	Damaged
14 Aug	PO D.M. Crook		
	& FO J.C. Dundas	He111	Destroyed
14 Aug	FO J.C. Dundas	Do17	Probable
16 Aug	FL P.C. Hughes	2 Me109s	Destroyed
16 Aug	Sgt P.K. Walley	He111	Probable (half share)
16 Aug	SL B.J.E. Lane	Me110	Damaged
16 Aug	PO E.S. Marrs	He111	Probable
18 Aug	Sgt P.K. Walley killed in action.		
18 Aug	PO E.S. Marrs	Ju87	Destroyed
18 Aug	FL P.C. Hughes	2 Me109s	Destroyed
18 Aug	FO W.H. Rhodes-Moorhouse	Me109	Destroyed
18 Aug	WC F.V. Beamish	Ju88	Probable
22 Aug	PO E.S. Marrs	Do17	Destroyed (half share)
24 Aug	WC F.V. Beamish	Do215	Damaged
24 Aug	SL B.J.E. Lane	Me110	Destroyed
25 Aug	PO E.S. Marrs	Me110	Destroyed
		Me110	Damaged
25 Aug	FO J.C. Dundas	Me110	Probable
26 Aug	FL P.C. Hughes	2 Me109s	Destroyed
29 Aug	PO R.H. Hillary	Me109	Destroyed
		Me109	Probable
30 Aug	FO W.H. Rhodes-Moorhouse	He111	Destroyed (third share)
30 Aug	WC F.V. Beamish	Me110	Probable
31 Aug	PO R.H. Hillary	Me109	Destroyed
31 Aug	FO W.H. Rhodes-Moorhouse	2 Me109s	Probables
31 Aug	FL M.L. Robinson	Me109	Destroyed
		Me109	Probable
		Me109	Damaged
2 Sep	PO R.H. Hillary	2 Me109s	Destroyed
		Me109	Probable
		Me109	Damaged
3 Sep	PO R.H. Hillary	Me109	Destroyed
	then shot down and badly burned.		
4 Sep	FL M.L. Robinson	Me110	Probable (half share)
4 Sep	FL P.C. Hughes	3 Me110s	Destroyed
4 Sep	FL W.H. Rhodes-Moorhouse	Do17	Destroyed
5 Sep	SL B.J.E. Lane	Me110	Destroyed
5 Sep	FL P.C. Hughes	2 Me109s	Destroyed
6 Sep	WC F.V. Beamish	Ju87	Destroyed
		Ju87	Probable
6 Sep	FL P.C. Hughes	Me109	Destroyed
		Me109	Probable

6 Sep	FO W.H. Rhodes-Moorhouse killed in action.		
7 Sep	FL P.C. Hughes	Do17	Destroyed
	then killed in action.		
7 Sep	SL B.J.E. Lane	Me110	Destroyed (third share)
11 Sep	WC F.V. Beamish	He111	Probable
11 Sep	SL B.J.E. Lane	Me110	Destroyed
		He111	Damaged
15 Sep	PO E.S. Marrs	2 He111s	Damaged
15 Sep	FO J.C. Dundas	Do17	Destroyed (third share)
		Do 17	Damaged
15 Sep	WC F.V. Beamish	He111	Probable
15 Sep	SL B.J.E. Lane	Do17	Destroyed (third share)
		Me109	Probable
17 Sep	PO E.S. Marrs	Ju88	Destroyed (third share)
18 Sep	WC F.V. Beamish	Me109	Destroyed
		Me109	Damaged
19 Sep	PO E.S. Marrs	Ju88	Damaged
24 Sep	FO J.C. Dundas	Me110	Destroyed
		Do17	Damaged
25 Sep	FL M.L. Robinson	Me110	Probable
25 Sep	PO E.S. Marrs	He111	Damaged
		Me110	Damaged
25 Sep	FO J.C. Dundas	Do17	Destroyed
26 Sep	FO J.C. Dundas	Me109	Destroyed
		Do17	Damaged
27 Sep	FO J.C. Dundas	Me110	Destroyed
27 Sep	PO D.M. Crook	Me110	Destroyed (half share)
30 Sep	PO D.M. Crook	2 Me109s	Destroyed
		Me109	Probable (half share)
30 Sep	FL M.L. Robinson	2 Me110s	Destroyed
		Me109	Destroyed
2 Oct	FO H.P. Blatchford	Do17	Destroyed (fourth share)
7 Oct	FL J.C. Dundas	Me110	Probable
7 Oct	SL M.L. Robinson	2 Me110s	Destroyed
12 Oct	WC F.V. Beamish	Me109	Damaged
15 Oct	FL J.C. Dundas	Me110	Destroyed
25 Oct	WC F.V. Beamish	Me109	Probable
		Me109	Damaged
30 Oct	WC F.V. Beamish	Me109	Probable
7 Nov	PO A.N.C. Weir killed in action.		
11 Nov	FL H.P. Blatchford	BR20	Destroyed
		CR42	Damaged
11 Nov	WC F.V. Beamish	CR42	Probable
13 Nov	WC F.V. Beamish	Me109	Damaged
14 Nov	PO E.S. Marrs	Ju88	Destroyed (half share)
15 Nov	SL B.J.E. Lane	Me110	Destroyed (third share)
17 Nov	FL H.P. Blatchford	Me109	Destroyed
27 Nov	FL J.C. Dundas	Ju88	Probable
28 Nov	PO E.S. Marrs	Me109	Destroyed
28 Nov	FL J.C. Dundas	Me109	Destroyed
	then killed in action.		

1941

Date	Name	Aircraft	Result
4 Jan	FO E.S. Marrs	Do17	Destroyed
10 Jan	WC F.V. Beamish	Me109	Destroyed
19 Mar	FL H.P. Blatchford	Ju88	Probable
7 May	SL M.L. Robinson	Me109	Damaged
8 May	SL M.L. Robinson	2 Me109s	Destroyed
12 May	FL H.P. Blatchford	He111	Destroyed
4 Jun	SL M.L. Robinson	Me109	Damaged (half share)
30 Jun	SL M.L. Robinson	Me109	Damaged
3 Jul	SL M.L. Robinson	2 Me109s	Destroyed
		Me109	Damaged
7 Jul	SL M.L. Robinson	Me109	Damaged
10 Jul	SL M.L. Robinson	Me109	Destroyed
11 Jul	SL M.L. Robinson	Me109	Destroyed
14 Jul	SL M.L. Robinson	Me109	Destroyed
18 Jul	FL E.S. Marrs	He111	Destroyed
18 Jul	SL M.L. Robinson	Me109	Damaged
24 Jul	FL E.S. Marrs killed in action.		
24 Jul	SL M.L. Robinson	Me109	Destroyed
		Me109	Damaged
7 Aug	SL M.L. Robinson	Me109	Probable
9 Aug	GC F.V. Beamish	Me109	Probable
		Me109	Damaged
24 Aug	WC M.L. Robinson	Me109	Destroyed
27 Aug	WC M.L. Robinson	Me109	Destroyed

1942

Date	Name	Aircraft	Result
13 Feb	GC F.V. Beamish	He114	Destroyed (shared)
9 Mar	GC F.V. Beamish	FW190	Destroyed
26 Mar	GC F.V. Beamish	FW190	Destroyed
		Me109	Destroyed
28 Mar	GC F.V. Beamish killed in action.		
10 Apl	WC M.L. Robinson killed in action.		
13 Dec	SL B.J.E. Lane killed in action.		

1943

Date	Name	Aircraft	Result
8 Jan	FO R.H. Hillary killed in flying accident.		
18 Mar	WC H.P. Blatchford	FW190	Destroyed
		FW190	Probable
4 Apl	WC H.P. Blatchford	2 FW190s	Damaged
2 May	WC H.P. Blatchford	FW190	Probable
3 May	WC H.P. Blatchford killed in action.		

1944

Date	Name	Aircraft	Result
18 Dec	FL D.M. Crook killed in flying accident.		

INDEX

Index